Stalking the Wild Dik-Dik

One Woman's Solo
Misadventures
Across Africa

Marie Javins

SEAL PRESS

Stalking the Wild Dik-Dik
One Woman's Solo Misadventures Across Africa

Copyright © 2006 Marie Javins

AVALON
publishing group incorporated

Published by
Seal Press
An Imprint of Avalon Publishing Group, Incorporated
1400 65th Street, Suite 250
Emeryville, CA 94608

ISBN-13: 978-1-58005-164-4
ISBN-10: 1-58005-164-2

9 8 7 6 5 4 3 2 1
Library of Congress Cataloging-in-Publication Data

Javins, Marie.
Stalking the wild dik-dik : one woman's solo misadventures across Africa / Marie Javins.
p. cm.
ISBN-13: 978-1-58005-164-4
ISBN-10: 1-58005-164-2
1. Africa—Description and travel. 2. Africa—Social conditions—1960-
3. Africa—Social life and customs. 4. Javins, Marie—Travel—Africa.
5. Women—Travel—Africa. I. Title.

DT12.25.J38 2006
916.04'33092—dc22
[B]
2006021110

Cover and interior design by Domini Dragoone
Printed in the United States of America by Malloy
Distributed by Publishers Group West

For my mother, Linda Walcroft,
who is always left holding the bag—
or, in this case, the goatskin lunch box—
while I'm off traipsing around the world.

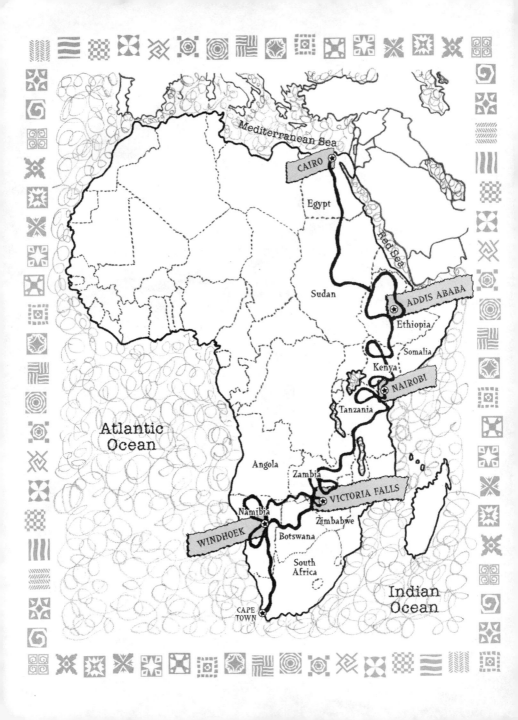

Contents

Introduction

In January of 2001, I believed that intimacy and codependence were the devil. They'd sneak up, perhaps through a few clever jokes. The jokes would turn into dates, and dates into weekends, time spent getting to know the other's family and friends. I'd seen it happen to many of my friends, one by one. They'd think someone was cute and next thing you know, they'd be moving to the suburbs with a spouse, two children, a dog, and an SUV. They'd once had other plans, but they couldn't recall them. They hated their jobs—who didn't?—but they'd be chained to the career ladder for life, for the kids, for the mortgage, for lack of a more imaginative approach to living.

I'd been on a lot of first dates through the last several years but not on a lot of second dates. I was adamantly independent, had other things on my mind, and dates were just the tempting bait in life's cleverest trap. I had a little travel problem, almost an addiction, that didn't leave room for life's trap. It wasn't about the destinations— it was about my reaction to new situations. Traveling made me improvise, think on my feet, and keep my mind wide open. Thanks to a tolerant boss and a freelance contract, I was able to work extra hard for ten months a year, getting ahead on my contract and taking two months off to visit exotic locales.

Problem was, I was slaving away miserably—mindlessly coloring and editing comic books as I had for more than a decade—for those ten months to enjoy the two months abroad. Something was obviously wrong with this.

I'd started to send travel diaries in '96 when I'd been in Central America, and I expanded them to an ambitious website in '98 with an eight-week trip across the Asian subcontinent and Middle East. This was with preblogging software, before the term "blog" even existed. I'd code the HTML in Notepad or SimpleText, upload it however I could, and add a few jpegs from photos hastily scanned in an Internet café. Digital cameras were not yet common.

Keeping an online diary meant I didn't have to bore friends who were not interested with the stories of my travels. Only those who genuinely wanted to see my holiday photos would look. Many people listen and look only to be polite, as they are more interested in their own lives than in mine (funny how that works). But there are others—total strangers—who relish tales of faraway lands. People I knew started forwarding my emails to people I didn't know. I started getting responses from strangers. The readers who enjoyed the stories the most were the ones with no hope of ever leaving home, the ones without passports or money, or they were people who used to travel but who were now disabled.

I'd just returned home from Southeast Asia in March of 2000. I sat with my mother, uncle, and aunt at a picnic table outside a restaurant. We talked of the trip I'd just had, my dissatisfaction with my ten-months-on, two-months-off lifestyle, and of my plans. What, we wondered, could I do on a grander scale to get me out of the repetitive job I was in once and for all?

Perhaps, I mused, I could go as far away on Earth as I could. To the opposite side of the planet from New York City, which was Australia. Then I'd have to get home by any means possible but would be forbidden to get on an airplane. That could be a good story to have up on the website. Surely that would be good enough for some articles and maybe even a book.

I started to research ships to see if it was possible to get out of Australia or if my plan would be a bust from the beginning.

What this research told me was that it was tough to leave Australia heading west but easy to get there from the east. So easy, in fact, that I could cover half the world in one Amtrak journey from New York to Los Angeles, followed by a ship voyage from Long Beach to Melbourne. Why do half the world when I could go around the whole thing simply by adding an extra month of easy travel?

And so MariesWorldTour.com was born. I'd go around the world in a calendar year, and I'd do it live, on the Internet. I'd go without airplanes, but I wouldn't stubbornly stick to that in emergencies. I'd send readers souvenirs from their virtual tour, and readers could vote on my route and excursions.

Richard Starkings of Comicraft liked the idea and offered to host my site. His designer, John "JG" Roshell of Active Images, was game. Friends contributed artwork and some travel outfitters offered discounts (and a few freebies). I sold my East Village condo, bought when the neighborhood was considered dicey and sold at what seemed then to be its trendy height. I'd have to live out of a backpack—and by my wits—for a year across Australia, Asia, Russia, Europe, Africa, and North America.

The plan was to get across Australia, Europe, and North America as quickly as possible. Things running smoothly and easily is not the stuff of good travel stories. No one wants to read about taking a walking tour of Rome's Colosseum or viewing the Rockies from a train window. No, the good stories happen when things go wrong. The more horribly wrong, the better the story.

I sleepwalked through most of Asia, having been there just one year before. Russia went smoothly, but Central Asia was a challenge. Uzbekistan was particularly difficult. But Africa—I loved Africa. So much so that I went back there to live for half of 2005. Parts of Africa look like what they call "aid porn," those starving-children-in-huts images we've seen on TV that tug at our hearts. But what these commercials don't show you is the dignity of the people living in the huts, how they live their lives with the same hopes and dreams for their families as those in the "developed" countries of the North. The images don't show the vibrant cities of Cape Town, Kampala, or

Nairobi. They don't imply that much of Africa also features flushing toilets, shopping malls, and gas stations just like in Ohio, or that genuine human concern for life is found in villages made of mud and sticks, the kind of concern that is lacking in the hypersocieties I'd lived in.

Parts of Africa are a hassle to navigate on public transport. Touts can be relentless in tourist areas, and tribalism often ruins otherwise healthy political systems. Crime rates are infamous in South Africa, people are starving from politically induced famine in Zimbabwe, and populations across the continent have been devastated by HIV. But life can also be a grand adventure in Africa, and while challenging, it can also be a rewarding place to live or travel in.

Crossing Africa in that year of 2001 taught me a lot about myself, and somewhere between Cape Town and Cairo—when I'd eaten my 250th meal of the year alone—I started to grasp something. I had met some fantastic people during the year. Some of them had enhanced my adventures and broken through my invisible barrier of solitude. Maybe—just maybe—it was possible to let my guard down. Maybe dates didn't have to turn into the ball and chain of a traditional life. Maybe I'd had it all wrong, and opening up to other people didn't automatically equal a miserable life of routine and a desk job.

But it would take me several more years of alienation and hard lessons—followed by months of living in Uganda, Namibia, and South Africa—before I fully understood this.

Marie
May 2006

Chapter 1

Curse
of the
Hippo

No, not that bump. Please don't drive there. I was sending mental instructions to my *boda boda*—or motor-scooter taxi—driver, who was cheerfully ignoring Kampala's potholes. *Not this bump either, please, no!*

I was sick and miserable. I'd woken up two nights ago with diarrhea, vomiting, fever, joint pain, and a host of other less-than-pleasant symptoms. My stomach felt as if I'd swallowed a hot-air balloon. I'd worried briefly about the proximity of the night clerk, whose office was next to my bathroom.

No one should have to listen to this, I thought.

But there was no time for regrets between my frequent visits to the bathroom that night.

Did I have malaria? Every faint flulike illness must be treated with great seriousness in Africa. Especially as I was on doxycycline as a prophylaxis, and this would mask many symptoms—although nothing seemed masked at the moment.

I spent the day as a sick day should be spent—lying on the sofa in front of the television. My stomach looked like the bloated stomachs you used to see on kids on those TV ads asking viewers to sponsor African children, the ones some cynics call "aid porn."

Finally, there was nothing left in my system save a little flat Coke that I'd been consuming. I was in Bbunga, a village on the outskirts of Kampala. When I'd rented this inexpensive long-stay corporate apartment far from the city center, it seemed a sensible financial decision. After all, I was in Kampala only half the time, and I spent the rest of my three-month stay in Uganda with my Bavarian boyfriend, who was working on location at an international-development assignment in Murchison Falls National Park, near the border of Congo. Now, the expat clinic and international hospital both seemed terribly far away. I didn't think I could make it to either without my guts exploding.

I gingerly walked up the road to a tiny, rundown clinic in the center of Bbunga.

"I'd like a malaria test, please."

A slow, sullen Ugandan man pricked my finger and dropped the blood on a slide. He went into the lab and gave it to an older man in a lab coat, who was busily playing computer solitaire. The door shut and I sat on an old chair in an unlit waiting area.

"You don't have malaria." The younger man came out with a piece of paper with a handwritten statement stating exactly that. I paid the fee of $1.20 and slowly, painfully began the short walk back home.

The next morning, I swallowed two Imodium tablets and braved the potholes. I had to see a doctor. A film canister was passed across the desk to me.

"Can you give us a stool sample?" the doctor asked.

"I took two Imodium," I responded, shrugging hopelessly.

He took back the film canister and suggested food poisoning as the culprit. I thought back on the carpaccio I'd picked at a few nights before at an upscale Italian restaurant in Kampala. And then I thought about Kampala's rampant power outages. Perhaps carpaccio had not been the wisest choice of starters. I hoped I'd be better in a few days. Herr Marlboro—the nickname I had given my boyfriend when I'd first met him years ago—was coming to Kampala. I was moving out of my accommodation and returning to Murchison Falls with him. We'd be parting for a while starting next week, when I'd head to Namibia and Cape Town before returning home to the States. His contract would keep him in Uganda for three more months. We'd had an idyllic summer together so far, our time split between the national park and Kampala. I didn't want to ruin our last week together by spending it lying on the sofa.

But I needn't have worried, as my food poisoning was low on the list of reasons my lover suddenly lost interest in me later that week. When he arrived in Kampala, he surprised me with a few tense discussions. But I had faith that things would work out—and he didn't know what else to do with me—so a few days later I was in Herr Marlboro's Toyota pickup truck on my way back to our national park home. We drove in near-silence, communicating only in strained, monotone sentences.

"Pull over," I said excitedly, breaking the mood with sudden enthusiasm.

He pulled up at a fruit-and-vegetable stand, where I wandered around buying tomatoes, pineapple, potatoes, onions, and bananas from pleased sellers. Once we were in the park, it was a long drive to the nearest large town, Masindi. I wanted to stock up on some of Uganda's plentiful fresh vegetables.

Happy with my purchases, I got back in the truck. H. M. turned the key in the ignition. Nothing happened. Well, something happened. Smoke rose from the fuse box under the hood.

The vegetable sellers watched as H. M. opened the hood and took out his mini-Leatherman multitool.

"Look," said H. M. as he pointed to a burned piece of plastic and metal. "Someone used a bridge and it's gone bad."

I nodded my agreement—pretending I understood—and left him to his work. I was a comic-book colorist and editor, but before he went into international development, H. M. had been a master auto mechanic near Munich. He was able to reroute a mystery cable from elsewhere to the starter. We could drive.

Unfortunately, the mystery cable turned out to charge the generator. We couldn't stop the car, as we didn't know if we had the battery power to start it again, and we had no lights. Murchison Falls is the largest national park in Uganda. Once we entered the national park boundaries, it was still another hour and a half to our three-bedroom house above the Nile. And the park is full of animals—

baboons, lions, owls, crocodiles, hippos, chimpanzees, elephants, giraffes, gazelles, and antelopes—and we wouldn't want to hit any of them because we were driving in the dark, plus it's illegal to go around driving into national park animals. We could not continue until morning.

We checked into a worn-out hotel in Masindi. Our little room was stiflingly hot and H. M. had a headache. He took a malaria self-test that came up negative. I knew that it was not malaria that was bothering him. It was me. His sickness was due to the stress of not knowing what to do about me. He carefully slept on his own half of the bed, while I stared at the ceiling fan. When I finally did sleep, I dreamed that my sister gave me a tiny St. Bernard puppy. I named it Masindi and took it for a walk downstairs from our hotel room. But I didn't know how to care for Masindi. I was careless and placed the puppy on the ground without a leash. A snake spied an opportunity and suddenly shot out of a hole in the ground. His jaws opened wide and he ate the puppy, while I stood there, helpless.

My final days at Murchison were not pleasant. We slept under a mosquito net on our screened veranda, as we always had. We listened for the hippo, which would come out of the Nile and into our yard at night to eat grass and flick his dung at our screen as he marked his territory. The park generators went off at midnight every evening, and then we'd look at the stars and listen to the frogs. But now, instead of taking pleasure in the incredible privilege of living in a national park in East Africa, we argued.

MariesWorldTour.com—my yearlong Internet-based trip around the world in 2001, with its lovely romantic evening on the Nile where we'd first met—played out its final chapter on the veranda one Tuesday night in late 2005. It wasn't a very nice ending.

I got up early and made breakfast for H. M., as one does when faced with cohabiting with someone right after everything has gone to hell. This set a more normal tone, but I was still surprised when he invited me on a game drive in late afternoon. Celsius—the park's electrician—was at the northern gate on the other side of the Nile. He needed a lift. We'd look at some animals en route. Celsius had been away for a few weeks, hosting his father's funeral. His father had been killed by LRA rebels north of Pakwach a few weeks ago. Killings were unfortunately a frequent occurrence in northern Uganda, where guerrillas calling themselves the "Lord's Resistance Army" have been murdering people and abducting children for indoctrination as soldiers for twenty years.

We loaded up on camera gear and off we went. But it was too hot for animals to be out in the sun. We saw nothing but a few gazelles.

After picking up Celsius and two others who were also hoping for a lift, we headed toward the ferry that would take us back across the Nile.

A hippo was eating grass in broad daylight at the ferry landing. Hippos usually stay in the water during the day, and I'd never seen a lone hippo grazing near humans. This large bull was covered in fresh scars, most likely from a territorial battle with another hippo. Maybe he'd wagged his tail and flicked his dung at the wrong spot, one already claimed by the shit of a bigger hippo.

H. M. grabbed his digital Canon and headed over. The hippo seemed used to people. Ranger cabins sat about fifty yards away and tourists were getting on and off the ferry. H. M. got closer than he normally would have. The hippo is the number-one human killer in Africa's animal kingdom. It is vegetarian but it has four-inch teeth, its mouth gapes 150 degrees, and it can run faster than a human. We liked having our yard hippo at Murchison Falls, but we respected it, just watching and listening when it came to visit us at night. But we'd also never had a chance to clearly photograph a hippo on land during daylight. H. M. hadn't been chomped yet, so I followed suit with my film Canon.

Click, whirr, went our cameras.

Then, through my 70-300 mm zoom lens, I saw the hippo stiffen and look up, his eyes looking directly at my camera. His face changed from "I like to eat grass" to "I will kill you, tourist." He charged. My shutter clicked.

H. M. and I turned and ran as one. Neither of us looked back or at each other. We were lucky to have twenty to thirty feet on the angry hippo, as he could easily have outrun us. I cradled my camera and was about to leap up on the pickup bed, while H. M. circled around to the other side of the cab. But the hippo had made his point. He'd slowed down and returned to eating grass.

Celsius was laughing at us from a distance. We joined in, full of adrenalin. We didn't really think the hippo could have killed us, as we had been close to the truck. But the awareness of death-by-hippo statistics was running through my head as I ran and I thought, *Stupid, Marie, very stupid.*

For a moment, all the tension of the past week was forgotten. Herr Marlboro and I laughed together as we crossed the Nile on the ferry. We touched for a moment, posing midriver while Celsius— holding the camera crooked—used up the last shot on my roll of film. I still had vain faith that things would work out. How could they not, I believed, with all of our history, romance, and similarities? Four years ago, we'd met in a most unlikely place as we both traipsed the back roads of the African continent. *There's no way it's ending with so much anger and disappointment,* I thought, *after such a romantic beginning, so long ago, at the end of a marathon journey from Cape Town to Cairo.*

Chapter 2

Crazy Like a Kudu

"You will like Cape Town," said the security guard at the container port. "It is a beautiful city."

It was August 2001. I had just left the container ship and taken my first steps into Africa. In my imagination, this moment had been monumental and romantic, the highlight of my yearlong trip around the world. I was like one of the great explorers from the 1800s . . . I was Stanley! I was Livingston! I was Speke! I was . . . a thirty-five-year-old Marvel Comics colorist with a backpack who'd slogged her way across the United States, Australia, Asia, and Russia before getting on the Africa-bound ship fifteen days ago in Europe. I'd faced off against corrupt police in Uzbekistan, had my bag slashed in Mongolia, and been sexually harassed on the Trans-Siberian Railway. I'd marveled at Angkor Wat in Cambodia, the Great Wall in China, and the bronze Frank Zappa bust in Lithuania. All of this had given me great confidence and made me brave, but the truth is that I was a little scared of Africa because I wasn't sure how I was going to get around.

Guidebooks listed bus routes in Thailand, train times in Russia, and ferry timetables for Indonesia. It hadn't been easy to go around the world by surface transport, but information had never been in short supply about popular tourist routes. The lesser-known places had been tougher, but the tough parts never lasted long before I was back on the well-trodden paths, most of them clearly documented in my guidebook.

Africa, meanwhile, had huge numbers of tourists visit parts of it every year. But most of these would go on safari trucks and overland tours, with good reason. You can't walk into national parks full of lions, and the public bus would get no closer to the Big Five—the vaunted sightings of lion, leopard, buffalo, elephant, and rhino—than the front gate. Most tourists go to Africa to go on safaris, not to catch minibuses that travel between cities.

Information was scarce for my trip northward by public transport. The south was easy—luxury buses plied the major highways of South Africa and Namibia, my chosen route on the way to Victoria Falls. But once I crossed the Zambezi River at Victoria Falls, everything would change. Listings in guidebooks and on the Internet were vague. "Daily bus leaves when full from lot by supermarket, except for buses that leave from dirt lot by T-junction." "Trains leave twice weekly and take between 36 and 52 hours." But one thing I'd learned from traveling the rest of the world was that in places where there are few private cars, people still have to get around. In theory, once I crossed the Zambezi, there'd be hundreds of local buses, the kind that leave when full. A string of these local buses would—I hoped—get me to Cairo in four months to catch my scheduled ship to Europe, where I—in spite of being a scruffy budget traveler—was scheduled to lecture on the December transatlantic *QE2* crossing. I'd promised my mother I'd be home by Christmas.

"You're American, aren't you?" The container-port security guard either made a lucky guess or one of the freight workers had told him. "I collect foreign currency. My collection is missing a dollar bill from the United States. If you have one, I could put it on my wall."

Yeah, right, I thought. But I appreciated his brazen attitude, so I grinned at him—but offered nothing—as he buzzed me through the gate and into Cape Town. It felt more as if I were entering a pawnshop at home in New York than as if I were crossing the threshold of a new, exciting continent.

My Cape Town plans were no more exciting than my entrance. I needed to see a dentist for a dull ache that had started under a back tooth, get some vaccines, and buy camping gear. Cape Town is a city not entirely unlike the European cities I'd left fifteen days ago. I was eager to get out into less familiar environs. I flagged down a taxi and got in.

"How do you like Cape Town?" asked the driver.

"I can't see it," I replied. "It's night."

"Ah. Well, it's a beautiful city."

For the next three days, I wandered the busy streets of Cape

Town, caught the bus to the upscale Victoria and Albert Waterfront Mall, and made repeated trips to my shipping line's dentist—who gave me a list of his favorite places in Victoria Falls along with a filling. I caught the cable car to the top of Table Mountain to survey the expansive view of the mountains, the flats beyond, and the Atlantic Ocean. Three days later, I left the budget hotel where I'd been staying to board the overnight luxury bus for Windhoek. Maybe I'd see some elephants and rhinos in Namibia. Maybe I'd meet some Namibians. This was it, I realized. Finally. I was going to see something new and different, to immerse myself in cultures totally unknown to me, not just leave a container port to enter a familiar urban environment.

"Did you enjoy your stay?" asked the front desk clerk.

"Yes," I said, knowing what was expected of me. "Cape Town is a beautiful city."

"Where will you go now?"

"I am catching the bus to Namibia."

He sighed dreamily.

"Namibia is lovely," he said. "Once you go, you must always go back. The sun is very bright there. It will shine right into your heart."

Sun was completely lacking at 5:30 AM in the central Windhoek parking lot that doubled as a bus station. Ephraim—the driver from the Cardboard Box hostel—was there, wearing a stiff cardboard sandwich board that advertised the hostel. He gave me a lift. I wasn't staying at the hostel, but the Crazy Kudu budget camping safari company had arranged to pick me up there at nine.

Namibia is a huge country—more than three hundred thousand square miles—that is populated by about two million people. By contrast, Manhattan has nearly as many people, but they are crammed horizontally and vertically into twenty-four square miles.

Public transportation in Namibia is limited to major routes only. The cheapest way to get into the desert and national parks is to bring friends and split the cost of car rental. But I didn't have any friends in Africa, so I'd done the next best thing and rented friends by signing up for the camping safari. I'd go around Namibia in a van with ten other people and a guide.

Cardboard Box was having a typically chaotic hostel morning. Dozens of people whisked in and out of the kitchen, some with wet hair, some in shorts, others in pajamas. Everyone was grabbing a different kind of breakfast from his or her personal stash of food stored in different lockers—toast, cereal, or eggs. In the common room, books were scattered about, and backpacks were piled in the corner. A couple came out of the shower together, hand in hand, as a woman in her seventies sat at the dining room table and sipped tea. She had a gash on her forehead that was just beginning to heal. I heard her describing a car accident on one of Namibia's many gravel roads to a college-age backpacker.

A stocky, thirtysomething tanned man with sandy-blond hair and skinny ankles had just come alone out of a shower. He had a friendly, open face, and his wet hair was plastered onto his forehead.

"Are you Marie?" he asked.

"Yeah." I was startled. "How do you know that?"

"I saw your name on the list of people coming in this morning. My name is Shawn."

We chatted briefly, before someone called for Shawn and he wandered off. He left the hostel without saying goodbye. I was disappointed. After being alone for most of the year, I didn't really open up to other people, but surprisingly, I'd liked him instantly.

Just before nine, the Crazy Kudu van—pulling a trailer—showed up on the street in front of the hostel. The driver's-side door opened and suddenly I understood why Shawn had spotted my name on the list of people coming to the hostel that morning. He hopped out of the driver's seat. Shawn was the guide and driver on my ten-day camping trip.

A pastry truck pulled up in front of Cardboard Box. Its driver started to sell baked goods to travelers, the same way an ice-cream man would sell Popsicles at home.

"I love Namibia!" I declared. "Breakfast comes to you."

I was the last one to enter the van, and we quickly carried out introductions among ourselves. Besides Shawn, our group consisted of six Italians, a Swedish couple named Lars and Carina, me, and a Namibian I'll call Joe who worked for a Namibian tourism office in Germany.

Namibia seemed full of Germans. The country had been a German colony for thirty years, before World War I. Fifteen thousand Germans live in Namibia today, and German charter airlines bring in planeloads of German tourists throughout the year. Coastal towns have yearly Oktoberfests, German breweries, and architecture right out of Bavaria. About 30 percent of the Namibian population is believed to speak German, even though Afrikaans—spoken as a second language by many of the indigenous tribes—is the common language of most of the country, and English is the official language.

We drove along modern, paved highways on our way out of Windhoek, past a modern shopping complex, a KFC, an upscale casino, and some hotels.

When I'd thought of going to Namibia, I'd thought of tribes, deserts, elephants, and dirt roads. I hadn't thought of shopping malls, Germans, potable water, and pristine toilets. I felt foolish as I looked around at what looked like a typical industrialized country. Africa was challenging my preconceptions, and I still hadn't left the cities.

We stopped at a gas station—a large one with both diesel and gasoline pumps, a brightly lit convenience store, and an attached greasy spoon—and I went into the ladies' room. Modern, clean, flushing toilets, and no charge! I stuck my nose back in my guidebook, where I learned that South Africa had seized control of Namibia from Germany after World War I and hadn't let go until 1990. Namibia was one of the world's newest nations, but its roads and infrastructure were not built the day after it gained independence. They'd been built a long time ago under the apartheid South African government. I felt like a walking cliché, a goofy green traveler who assumed that going to Namibia was going out into "the bush."

My face felt hot with the shame of ignorance as I read on, learning that Namibian independence had been part of a regional UN peace deal that also included a settlement in the fighting between Angola and South Africa. I had known only the vaguest details about South Africa's support for one side during the Angolan war and was embarrassed by my unawareness—especially when I later read that

Angola had been as much a Cold War front as Vietnam had been. Cuba had supplied the Angolan side, while the United States had backed South Africa and the rebels fighting the Angolan government. Shawn—then a South African citizen—had spent three years in jail as a conscientious objector instead of going to war.

"What was jail like?" I asked him later, once we'd hit it off and I was regularly sitting in the front passenger seat.

"It wasn't that bad," said Shawn. "I learned to garden and cut hair."

He'd become a Namibian citizen after serving his time and had earned a degree in conservation. He'd then spent months alone in remote Namibian reserves, observing mongooses and counting zebras. He was freelancing for Crazy Kudu, and later he would try out running upscale safaris before settling down to manage luxury lodges across southern Africa.

We headed north through glaring sun and scrubby desert brush, through vast expanses of flat nothing interspersed with small towns of a few shops and one large gas station. Our group was silent behind sunglasses. We all stared out windows and sweated in the desert heat for five hours before stopping to camp overnight.

We had six tents to shelter the eleven of us. Shawn set up his air mattress and sleeping bag outside, giving Joe and me a tent each. We were the single travelers and would have been expected to share with each other if Shawn had slept in his own tent, as was standard practice for the group leader. Lars and Carina—both PhD candidates, one in molecular biology and the other in economics—erected their tent in record time. I pokily stuck a few poles together and stared at them. I'd stayed in cheap hotels and hostels throughout the rest of the world, and I hadn't set up a tent since I was a kid. Some world traveler I was—baffled by a few poles and canvas, right after silently acknowledging my total ignorance about the history and modern culture of southern Africa.

Maybe that hole in the canvas was for the end of a pole. OK, it fit. But then what?

Luckily for me, Lars and Carina were not just smart, they were also kind.

"It's much easier with two people," said Lars, pretending it wasn't my own ineptitude that made erecting a tent seem like rocket science. Carina helped while I memorized the motions. Poles go in little holes. Clips go on poles. Tie it at the top. It was surprisingly easy. Tent design had come a long way since I was a kid.

Dinner was steak and potatoes, cooked by Shawn on the campfire. I fetched some water for washing dishes. Maybe I could redeem myself for the tent episode by showing I was ready to help with the camp dishes. To my embarrassment, Shawn gently pointed out that the ablution block included not just men's and women's bathrooms, but also a small kitchen. We'd just wash our dishes in the sink, as if we were at home. And the women's room, which had several clean toilet stalls and showers, also featured bathtubs. Namibia was still surprising me.

The weather surprised me too. Hot by day, Namibia in winter got icy cold at night. I was glad for the fleece sleep sheet I'd bought in Cape Town.

Months later, when I was an expert camper with a great deal more knowledge of African history and social conditions, I'd look back sheepishly on my early days in Africa. But Namibia was a good country to start with. "It's Africa for beginners," a German tourist declared to me later. I didn't know it at the time, but I was easing myself slowly into a tough trip northward.

We broke camp and drove on in the morning, stopping in the small town of Otjiwarongo for groceries. Something wet was dripping from underneath the van.

"I thought they fixed that," muttered Shawn to himself. It was steadily leaking gas. Shawn didn't seem too bothered by the discovery, and he momentarily disappeared back into the grocery store. He returned with a bar of soap and some sugar, which he kneaded together in his hands, massaging it into a thick ball. He disappeared under the van to paste this concoction over the hole in the gas tank. I was impressed. Competence and confidence always impress me.

In early afternoon, we pulled into Etosha National Park. The reserve—which is about the size of New Jersey—is one of the world's top game reserves, but being in a relatively new country, it is nowhere near as famous as its cousins Kruger, Serengeti, or Masai Mara. I proudly set up my tent alone this time, glad to have acquired a new skill that would turn out to serve me well in the coming years.

We raced through a lunch of cucumber and cold lunch-meat sandwiches before heading out for a game drive.

We drove less than three minutes before a giraffe practically walked up, smiled, and said, "Cheese."

"*Bellissimo!*" murmured an Italian.

Shutters clicked from the seats behind me. We were all amazed, as our normal daily encounters with animals would have involved dogs, cats, and pigeons.

"Look, zebras!" Zebras traveled in groups of hundreds, sticking close together to ward off predators. Then we spotted various antelope-like creatures: oryx, springbok, and some decidedly *un*-crazy kudu, identifiable by their shaggy coats and spiraling horns.

Next up were warthogs, looking like proud, tan pigs with tusks and shaggy heads of hair, followed by tremendous herds of giraffes, their long necks towering above the desert.

"What's that?" I pointed to what looked like a chihuahua, but which had Bambi ears and hooves and an oversize head with cartoony eyes and sultry eyelashes. The little chihuahua blinked once—it seemed to be flirting with me.

"A dik-dik." Shawn laughed. "It's a kind of antelope. They travel in pairs. Let's find the other dik-dik."

The mate was nearby, almost obscured by a bush. The tiny dik-dik does a lot of hiding behind bushes. Any animal that wakes up with a craving for meat can eat a dik-dik, unless it finds a good hiding place.

The benefit of Etosha is that you can see its wildlife clearly. Namibia is a desert country, and while other game reserves feature lush, green landscapes brimming with trees and vegetation, Etosha is a flat salt pan that offers little cover for the dik-dik and all its fellow animals. But the fact it's a desert does not mean nothing lives here. Etosha has water, and water holes mean wildlife.

We headed back to camp a few hours later, and I walked over to the local water hole. The whole campsite was fenced in, but one section had small bleachers overlooking a water hole just outside the fence. I sat with other tourists and watched for a long time.

Only birds came to drink.

Our evening drive was not fruitful either. We pulled up at one water hole, wondering why so many cars were parked there. Could these people all be staring at the sole thirsty zebra?

No. They weren't watching anything. Everyone was just waiting, hoping that some animals would come to drink. We sat in a crowd of ten cars, all staring at nothing.

A Namibian school bus full of children pulled up. The driver looked at me and mouthed, "What?"

"Nothing," I mouthed back, shrugging. He laughed and drove his bus away.

After staring at nothing for twenty minutes, we gave up and headed back to camp. At dinner, over beef stew, Shawn told us stories of traveling on a Namibian passport. He had been strip-searched at airports and treated with disdain by people who had never heard of his country. In the United States, an African American had refused to believe that Shawn was African.

"But I am African," Shawn told him. "I'm more African than you are!"

The man had been astonished. I was too. Embarrassed again by my ignorance, I pretended I had realized how diverse the population of southern Africa was. I'd known that South Africa was diverse, but since arriving I'd also met white Namibians and transplanted white Kenyans. Soon enough, I would meet white Zimbabweans and Asian Ugandans.

After dinner, Joe—the Namibian tourism officer—angrily erupted with a viewpoint I hadn't heard before.

"Marie, do you see these overland trucks?" he asked, motioning toward the nearby groups and their large vehicles. "What kind of people go on vacations for months?"

I didn't realize the question was rhetorical, and I tried to answer him honestly.

"Many of them are students, or people who are changing jobs, getting divorced, or going through a lifestyle change. Lots of them just want to travel without spending too much money."

Joe wasn't interested.

"Why would they go for months in such a vehicle? Don't they want jobs?"

He obviously had missed the discussion in which I'd told the group that I was without job, home, or income and was traveling the world to write about it on the Internet.

"How much does it cost?" he asked, still obsessed with overland trucks.

"The longest trips go for nine months and can cost upward of $10,000," I answered. I'd been on two overland trucks before, one in the Middle East and one in Central America, and had written a few articles on the subject.

This outraged Joe.

"Don't they have anything better to do? Why don't they give their money to charity?"

I had no answer for that.

We all headed back to the floodlit water hole for more nocturnal animal-watching. The animals were mostly small antelopes and I decided to go take a shower while everyone else was busy.

"I'll walk back to camp with you," said Shawn. He'd seen a lot of animals in his time.

I showered and headed back to the campsite. The others had not returned yet, and Shawn had finished his chores. He sat at a picnic table, drinking a beer.

"All clean?"

"Yeah." It was a pleasure to be clean in the dusty desert. "But it's so dry here. I need some moisturizer. Especially for my feet! They feel like snakeskin."

"I have some moisturizer in the van." Shawn got it and offered it to me as he examined my sandal-clad snakeskin-style feet. "They look pretty bad," he said.

He then told me about the reflexology class he'd taken in Cape Town.

"You want me to show you? I could use the practice."

Not one to say no to a foot rub, I said, "Sure." I enjoyed it, but I was petrified. I didn't want to be the cliché—the single woman desperately chasing the guide. And for all I knew, Shawn did this to all the single women on his trips. I was relieved when Lars and Carina walked up, and Shawn stopped quietly, pulling his hands back. I was not in the habit of letting total strangers rub my feet. Surely Shawn was not lying that he had taken the reflexology class. But surely rubbing dirty feet that had been in Tevas all day could not be that entertaining. *He was probably hitting on me. Or was he?*

Shawn's own feet were on display early the next morning, when he oddly wore no shoes as he served breakfast. Afterward, we packed up our gear. I had gotten as good at taking my own tent down as I was at putting it up. We were ready to go, but Shawn was missing. Then he trotted up in his sandals.

"A jackal stole my shoes while I was sleeping," he said. The fence kept big predators outside the campground, but smaller animals could still get in. The jackal hadn't gone far before discovering that shoes were not very tasty. Shawn had scoured the surrounding area until he found the missing sandals.

I felt guilty; Shawn was sleeping outside to give me my own tent.

Shawn drove us toward Okaukuejo Rest Camp to spend a night in the western part of Etosha. Okaukuejo is the park's research point and—like all Etosha's campgrounds—sits next to a permanent water hole that is floodlit at night. Perhaps this nocturnal viewing, forty miles from our first campsite, would produce different wildlife.

We stopped for breakfast in a fenced-in area with a picnic table and two outhouses. The humans in Namibian game parks are fenced in, while the animals roam freely. A few years later, I'd find myself explaining to a native Namibian woman that there are no fences around the camping and picnic areas in East Africa, that the people sleep in tents out in the bush, and that the lions ignore them. She'd accuse me of lying.

"Are you on a special diet or something?" asked Joe. I was eating my usual breakfast of Oats So Easy instant oatmeal from an envelope, while everyone else ate cereal with milk.

"I can't have dairy," I explained.

"Can you have goat's milk?" he asked.

"Yes."

"Marie, the next time you come to Namibia you must visit my village. I will reserve a special goat just for you."

We drove off, passing giraffes, oryx, springboks (springing

wildly in a gait called "pronking"), warthogs, elephants, and zebras (pronounced *zeh*-bra outside of the States). We stopped at one water hole crowded with wildlife and sat in the van staring intently. We'd quit noticing the plentiful animals through sheer, overwhelming volume, but perhaps we'd see something new?

Carina studied a vulture through her binoculars and saw a movement just north of it.

"What is that?" she wondered aloud. "Is it . . . ? *Yes,* it is! It is a lion!"

Sharp-eyed Carina had spotted a waving tail. Upon closer inspection, we discovered that the tail was attached to a lioness, who was lazing about with three of her relatives.

The lioness got up slowly and padded toward the water hole. Every animal nearby snapped to attention. Springboks and zebras alike froze and watched. Now was not the time to give in to thirst.

One cheeky warthog decided to have a drink. He trotted bravely up to the pool. The lioness's head turned slightly toward him. Without changing her speed, she nonchalantly started to move in his direction, stalking cagily.

We all got excited. We hurriedly changed camera lenses. After a buzzing of murmurs, no voices could be heard as we waited in anticipation. I was rooting for the warthog. All the other animals had quit grazing and watched as we did, unmoving.

The warthog seemed to take only a few sips before strolling away at a more rapid clip than he'd used on his initial approach.

The lioness couldn't be bothered to follow. She lay down before reaching the water, playing it as if she didn't care for warthog steak anyway. The other animals moved again and went about their business, but they all gave the lioness a wide berth.

"I hate lions," Shawn said to me in a low voice. As one of two solo travelers and the person he'd talk to most, I'd become his codriver and was always in the front passenger seat. "Everyone wants to see lions, and they ignore all the birds and other animals. And sometimes we don't even see lions, and then everyone is disappointed."

"How many lions are there here?" I asked.

"Four to six hundred at last count, but they stray to kill cows because it's easy, and then farmers shoot them."

At the next water hole, Joe—our resident official—lost his temper. He was sure he'd seen someone step out of a car to snap a photo.

"Did you see that?" he said. "A man just got out of his car! If I had the papers, I'd fine him right now. These are wild animals. People should never get out of cars here."

He calmed down a minute later when Carina spotted a hyena loping across the plain.

"*Bellissimo!*" said an Italian.

"Look, there's more. Maybe they're going in for a kill," said someone. "Oh, wait, no, that's an oryx, not a hyena."

We continued to Okaukuejo. Our campsite's world-famous water hole features a webcam and rhino visits in addition to nocturnal viewing. We sat on benches for hours that evening, watching animals come to drink. We saw black rhinos, some of which made odd bleating sounds while sparring.

"I've never heard a rhino make that noise before," said Shawn, astonished.

A breeding herd of ten elephants dropped by, along with the usual springboks and one old, farting elephant. The old elephant was alone, a tribeless renegade.

The Okaukuejo water hole attracts hundreds of human visitors a day, and not all are respectful of the QUIET, PLEASE sign. It was incongruous to watch rhinos and elephants while I breathed secondhand smoke and listened to beer-guzzling, chatting tourists.

Dinner was spaghetti, which afforded the Italians ample opportunity to declare "needs more salt" and "not enough garlic."

Afterward, we sat by the fire and chatted.

The others turned in, but I stayed up, eager to help Shawn with his reflexology practice, which I justified by thinking, "If he wants to rub my filthy feet, he's welcome to it."

We broke camp early the next morning and headed west down dirt roads to the desert and Damaraland.

Most of the group fell asleep. There was no reason not to. The scenery was repetitive—dirt, sand, and scrub brush. Whenever a car approached, we rolled up windows to avoid the inevitable trail of dust that followed. We were all tired and filthy when we reached our lunch stop at the Petrified Forest.

Shawn gave Lars $20 Namibian and instructed him to pay the guide at the end of the tour. Guides were compulsory, as the Namibian government didn't want tourists carrying off bits of 260 million-year-old tree trunks.

Unfortunately, Petrified Forest guides were renowned for their uselessness. Ours was apparently more energetic than most as he spoke about eight sentences instead of the usual one or two.

"This is the long one," explained our guide, pointing to an especially long piece of petrified wood.

"This is the big one." This wood was wider than the others.

"This is the nice one." The guide pointed to another piece, not discernibly different from the others.

Joe, meanwhile, was outraged over the guide's pay.

"Marie, don't you think that Shawn's company could afford to pay this man more than three US dollars?" he asked.

"I don't know, Joe," I said, noncommittally. But I did know. The going rate was $1.25, so we were already overpaying. The guide, meanwhile, lived up to the reputation for uselessness, and I wasn't sure we should even have bothered with the Petrified Forest.

Joe gave $20 Namibian of his own to Lars.

"Please give him this as well." Lars agreed with reluctance.

The guide pretended to be oblivious to the discussion about money going on around him, but he did then strike up a conversation with Joe.

"Do you work for the company?" asked the guide.

"No," said Joe. "I am a tourist."

"Oh. What country are you from?"

Joe found this hilarious.

"I am from Namibia!"

Joe pulled me aside later.

"Marie, do you know why the guide asked me where I am from?"

"Um, because if you were Namibian you wouldn't go to the Petrified Forest on a tour? You'd just go there in a car?"

"No. It is because Namibians don't do this. They are not tourists. They do other things, like spend time with their families or work."

After lunch, we drove on, past hand-painted PETRIFIED FOREST signs that offered two or three pieces of wood and little competition for the scintillating real thing. Our route took us near Twyfelfontein and then south down the Skeleton Coast—so named for the bleak, rocky coast that is dotted with shipwrecks—to Swakopmund. We stopped at Cape Cross en route to see the enormous seal colony there. I also encountered my first and only dirty toilet in Namibia there. But the smell of the dirty toilet was a good match for the overbearing smell of seal excrement. Thousands of fur seals were plopped on the beach just on the other side of a low wall, and thousands of fur seals don't hang around and bark together without generating some serious stink. They ignored the smell as much as they ignored us tourists, seeming to be far more interested in basking, scratching, or dragging themselves along the beach on their little handlike flippers.

"I'm excited to do my laundry," I said as we approached Swakopmund. "And to go to the camera store. And to wash my hands."

"I'm excited not to have to pump up my bed," said Shawn.

Joe left us at a gas station in Swakopmund. He'd had enough touring and was catching a minibus back to Windhoek. The rest of us were staying in A-frame chalets at the Swakopmund Rest Camp. The six Italians took one chalet (jokingly calling it Little Italy), while the other four of us spread around the remaining six-person A-frame.

I had to run a few errands in town, and Shawn was going to the launderette. He offered to do my laundry, too. I felt weird handing my dirty underwear to a man I'd been flirting with all week, but he didn't seem to mind doing my laundry any more than he minded rubbing my filthy feet every night.

Lars and Carina took the double room downstairs while Shawn and I had beds in the loft on the second floor. Shawn crossed the loft and sat on my bed. We were silent, both waiting for the other one to address the obvious attraction between us.

"Marie, this doesn't happen," he explained to me as we eyed each other like two dik-diks that had just met. "I don't get involved with clients. It doesn't happen."

"Shawn, I'm leaving on Friday for Zimbabwe. I already have the bus ticket. I have to be there to join a safari to Botswana. I have a schedule to keep. For MariesWorldTour.com. For the website." I spoke gently. I sounded firm, as he had. But I didn't feel firm.

Shawn hugged me and kissed me on the cheek before walking across the loft to his own bed. *Should I call him back?* I did not. The website was just an excuse. My feelings were conflicted. I barely knew Shawn, and getting involved with a man in Namibia, only to leave immediately, seemed pointless. And while he was nice and funny, he had that invisible wall around him that people build when they don't have room for close relationships. I knew the symptoms well. I had my own wall. That wall was what made it easy for me to move from town to town, from group to group. I'd started young, developing a thick skin in my teenage years when my family had problems with harassment from substance-abusing neighbors. Those neighbors had taken great amusement in things such as hooting at passers-by, consuming copious amounts of beer on the lawn all night, and trying to burn down our house. It had been a case of toughen-up-or-wilt. I believed that keeping a distance was essential to the lifestyle I'd chosen.

People who worked in tourism made new friends constantly, only to find themselves deserted on a predictable schedule when the new friends' holidays ended. Shawn had new friends leave him every ten days. He'd earned his loneliness, and I had no right to tamper with it unless I was prepared to stay. And I was not ready to dismantle my own wall of solitude yet. Not for years.

I lay there in bed, thinking of Turbo in Australia (every Aussie male seems to have multiple nicknames). I couldn't picture his face any more. I'd met him in China in April, and he'd been waiting for me since then. I'd agreed to join him in New South Wales in January when my trip ended.

I shut out the temptation across the loft and went to sleep.

The next day was adventure activity day in Swakopmund. Actually, every day in Swakopmund was adventure activity day, but today was special because we were able to take advantage of it. Swakopmund—one of the most German towns in Namibia—had become the organized adventure capital of the region, second only to Victoria Falls, Zimbabwe. In Swakopmund, you can quad-bike over dunes along the ocean in the morning, jump out of a plane over the desert in the afternoon, ride a horse or camel at sunset, and watch a video of your day later at the bar. If you're too tired for all that activity, you can lie on the beach, visit the uranium mine, or go on a dolphin-viewing cruise.

Lars and Carina went shark-fishing. The rest of us signed up for an authentic Swakopmund sport, practiced in only a few places worldwide: Sand-boarding! It wasn't something I'd dreamed of doing, but it was what people did when they came to Namibia.

A van from the local Adventure Center carried us out to the

dunes. I was disappointed when Shawn stayed behind to patch—again—the ever-widening hole in the Crazy Kudu van's gas tank.

I began to doubt the wisdom of my joining the expedition as we trudged up the enormous sand dunes. We were all wearing helmets and gloves and carrying flimsy pieces of three-foot-long particleboard. Our feet sunk into the sand as we clumsily struggled up a hundred-foot dune.

Breathless and swearing quietly, I arrived at the top of a massive dune that I was now expected to go down before climbing up again. The problem with sand-boarding, I realized, was not going down the dunes. It was going back up.

One by one, we sledded down the dunes. To slow down, we'd drag our feet. To go faster, you just go down a steeper dune. Fine particles of sand filled my shoes and covered my hair. We learned we could whiz down the dunes at speeds of up to forty miles per hour, though I dragged my feet enough to slow down just a little. It was a thrill, though I was breathless in the hot sun and quickly assigned myself the job of group photographer to avoid too many trips up and down.

Shawn showed up in time for the tandem ride. Two went on each board.

I snuggled up behind Shawn on a board, and I am embarrassed to report that my inferior sand-board–navigation skills caused us to wipe out dramatically.

"Both hands!" yelled Shawn, referring to our rudder—my gloved hands, which dragged behind us in the sand.

A second later, I daintily slid off onto my bottom. Shawn fared worse—he managed to do several 360-degree turns on his way down the dune. He landed on his face, laughing, though the wipeout must have been painful.

After lunch and a shower—during which I noticed I sported horrible bruises from the sand-boarding—I strolled around quirky Swakopmund, checking out the asparagus at the *frische spargel* stand, passing by the butcher's shop to contemplate today's specials, which were *Gulasch mit Nudeln und Salat* and "kudu salami." I window-shopped, checking out the German-language books at the bookstore and the African craft stores, which all seemed to sell the same T-shirts, wooden carvings, and safari hats. Later, Shawn joined me for a sunset drink at a seaside restaurant set on the edge of Swakopmund's municipal beach.

"This is the best view of the sunset in town," he said. We walked along the shore afterward, alongside charming vacation homes and seafood restaurants. Swakopmund, with its palm trees and German bakeries, deserved more than a day and a half. I promised myself that I'd be back.

In the morning, we collected a new passenger to replace Joe before driving south along dusty dirt roads toward the dunes at Sesriem, passing through the port town of Walvis Bay on the way. Walvis Bay was—until the mid-'90s—a small outpost of South Africa in the middle of Namibia.

The sun glared, too bright to be dimmed even by the sunglasses each passenger wore. The scenery was so repetitive—dusty, brown, and yellow, with small shrubs poking out of the sand—that it was impossible to stay awake. Only Shawn kept his eyes open all day.

As usual, the drive and the campsite were both dusty and hot.

It's part of being a tourist in the desert. Being outside a tent meant getting dirty. Being inside a tent required being outside in order to get inside, which meant getting dirty. I was now constantly filthy and was regularly having to eat processed lunch meat. Even worse, I was looking forward to it.

The requisite six or more overland trucks dotted the campground, but we scored a prime spot with easy access to the two ablution blocks.

We were to leave at 5:15 AM. The point was to be first in line at the gate to the dunes, so that we wouldn't be stuck in line behind dozens of overland trucks.

Sunrise at Sesriem is one of the prime attractions in Namibia. Sunrise is when all the interesting shadows are cast across the orange-red dunes, but the gate to the park itself doesn't open until 5:30. It's sixty-five kilometers from the gate to the dune parking lot, and then, unless you have a 4WD vehicle that can handle sand, you have to hike the last four kilometers to the biggest dune—or Sossusvlei—from there.

"Given the time the gates open and the distance involved," Shawn had told us, "it's actually impossible to get to the top of Sossusvlei by sunrise. Just get as close as you can and then scramble up any available dune."

There was only one hitch. At 5:30, we were still at camp.

Two of the Italians were missing. And the sun wasn't going to wait.

Finally, they showed, strolling casually from their morning ablutions.

"For God's sake, get in. We're fifteen minutes late!" Carina gave them a tongue-lashing. Cowed by her anger, they jumped in the van and we raced to the gate. We'd missed the line, but the guard insisted on making sure that all the Crazy Kudu paperwork was in order. Shawn fidgeted as we waited.

Then we joined the daily Sossusvlei Rally, already in progress.

Zoom! We passed an overland truck. And then raced past another. Shawn was used to being first in the Sossusvlei Rally and he wasn't going to let a late start keep him back.

Ahead, we saw a white van, identical to our own save for the "Wild Dog" logo on the side. Wild Dog was Crazy Kudu's main competition in the Namibian budget-safari business, though they merged four years later.

"Should I take the Dog?" asked Shawn.

"Take the Dog! Take the Dog!" we yelled.

He dusted the Dog. We pulled into the Sossusvlei parking lot five minutes ahead of the nearest competitor.

"First again," declared our cocky would-be Wacky Racer.

We tourists piled out and briskly hiked down the sand road toward the biggest dune of the pack. Actually, we didn't do anything briskly. Slogging four kilometers through thick sand can hardly be called brisk.

"Sossusvlei is the tallest dune, but they're all basically the same," said Shawn to me quietly. "Don't go up Sossusvlei. It's packed with people, the Disney World of dunes. Come with me and we'll look at Sossusvlei from a distance."

I followed Shawn off the track, cutting across the flat surrounding wilderness. He'd done this dozens of times and took me to a good spot for viewing the sunrise. I wore socks with my sandals since it had been cold in the morning and now Shawn mocked my lousy fashion sense. By now, we were friendly enough that I took his teasing with a laugh. We scrambled up the nearest dark dune and plopped onto the top to watch the morning brighten. As the sun rose, the dunes and the desert turned to rich orange. As the morning went on, the dunes lost their redness and changed to a paler yellow. In the distance, dozens of people were rushing up Sossusvlei, although the sun was now high in the sky.

We headed back to the parking lot early as Shawn had to lay out our breakfast of toast and cereal. He'd also put out a bowl of water, and birds flocked to it, desperate for a bit of moisture.

"Everyone feeds these birds," he said. "But no one thinks to give them water."

The next morning—the final day of my Crazy Kudu budget camping safari—Shawn got up early and made a new soap-and-sugar patch for the still-leaking gas tank. We tore down a gravel road, hoping the patch would get us back to Windhoek. The van was leaving on another ten-day trip in the morning and was scheduled to go in for a new gas tank the minute we pulled back into town.

The patch didn't hold, and the hole kept getting bigger. We pulled over constantly to add soap to the tank, and we filled it up with gas twice more. I tried to distract Shawn from worrying by asking him to teach me Afrikaans, but all I remembered afterward was that "buy a donkey" means "thank you very much."

The third time we pulled over to check the soap patch, I took the opportunity to go pee behind a rock. When I got back to the van, a new surprise awaited.

"You're not going to believe this, Marie," said Shawn. "We have a flat."

But the tire was changed quickly, and we drove on.

Leaking gas, tired, and hot, we finally hit paved road at the small, sun-drenched town of Rehoboth.

"This is a horrible town," said Shawn. "I had to work here for six months as part of my practicum, and on the first day someone asked me to shoot his dog."

He had told the man that he didn't have a gun and suggested he take his sick dog to the vet next door.

"A minute later, I heard a noise and went outside. They were chopping the dog's head off with a shovel." Shocked, I agreed that perhaps the town was not the nicest place.

The fuel gauge indicated that we had half a tank left as we pulled out of Rehoboth. We hemorrhaged fuel the last ninety kilometers to Windhoek and arrived at the Crazy Kudu office burning fumes.

The owner of Crazy Kudu walked up to the van as soon as we'd stopped. "Sorry we had to bring you all here but the van has a petrol leak."

Someone giggled. The rest of us stared at him in astonishment. We were, of course, aware of the leak, having each sweated it out for the last hour and a half as we'd all leaned over to keep our eyes on the fuel gauge.

We said our goodbyes and left in three separate Crazy Kudu vehicles. Shawn dropped both our packs at the Cardboard Box and then took me to dinner at Spur Grand Canyon restaurant, where a group of Namibian waiters dressed as Native Americans sang "Happy Birthday" to a little girl.

"The problem with MariesWorldTour.com," said Shawn over steak, "is that it gives you no flexibility. You have this bus ticket. You have this certain number of days and places to be. You have to move on."

I looked at my plate. I'd bought tonight's bus ticket weeks ago. But it wasn't just the ticket, or the Botswana safari I'd signed up for that began in a few day's time. No, it was my other concerns. Flirting was fun, but if I hung around, the temptation would beat my resolve.

Lars and Carina met Shawn and me at the bus stop later in the evening. Together, the four of us boarded the Intercape Mainliner bus for the nineteen-hour ride to Victoria Falls, Zimbabwe. Shawn sat next to me, holding my hand instead of my foot this time, and for once, I didn't pull it back. It hadn't been easy to get to know him with nine other people around, but he had become a friend and I would miss him. He left when the bus engine started, to the surprise of Lars and Carina.

"Shawn is not going with us?" They teased me with half smiles and gleams in their eyes.

No, he wasn't. I saw him through the tinted window—head down—walking away in the direction of the Cardboard Box. The walk sign flashed and he jogged a bit to cross the intersection before the light turned. I lost sight of him.

As the bus pulled out of Windhoek, I wondered if I'd made a mistake. Perhaps I'd been hasty in seizing the first opportunity to flee. But it would take him a visit to New York and me two visits to

Namibia before we were both in the same place at the same time again four years later in Cape Town. And even then, he would prove elusive, offering me the same subconsciously deliberate hurdles I'd used to fend him off in Namibia.

Chapter 3

Hell Hitch

I hated the town of Vic Falls, and the hostel I'd checked into was overland-truck hell.

Dozens of drunken overlanders had partied hard into the night. Other overlanders were up early, prepping trucks for departure.

The south and east of Africa is infested with overland trucks. I've taken these in other parts of the world and had a positive view of these miniworlds on wheels. About twenty tourists can ride in the back of the truck, which have comfortable bus-style seats, safes, and a drink cooler. African trips feature cooks, and there are always two staff members who can drive, repair the truck, and organize campsites and hotels. Luggage is kept in a secure locker, while food and spare parts ride underneath. Camping gear goes on top of the truck. Quite a sensible way to get from A to B in tricky parts of the world where one does not necessarily wish to travel alone. I'd taken one across Pakistan and Iran and loved it. I planned to take one into Ethiopia in a few months.

But in southern and eastern Africa, there are not one or two companies running trucks a few times a year. Dozens of competing companies keep trucks running full. As many as six trucks can congregate at a campground at one time, and the ensuing drunken mayhem can make it seem as if being in Africa is incidental. The fun is in the group.

Unless you are not in the group.

Shocked by the line for the toilet and alienated by the partiers, I walked to town to search for food. Touts and money changers eagerly rushed to meet me.

"Good morning," said a man who waved a fistful of necklaces in my face.

"No, thank you," I replied in a carefully rehearsed monotone.

Another man fell into step beside me.

"How are you?"

"No, thank you."

"I'm just trying to be friendly."

"No, thank you."

He gave up, but three more men were waiting just ten feet away.

"Change money," hissed the first.

"Good morning, just-my-size," said the second.

"*What??*" I stopped, appalled.

"Uh . . ." The second man hesitated. The third just smiled at the discomfort of his friend.

I turned down Livingstone Way. A man followed about six paces behind me.

"Sssst," he said. I ignored him.

"Sssst."

"Sssst." Surely he'd get bored.

"Sssst."

Three uniformed policemen stood just ahead. Perhaps now was a good time to stand up to the steaming-teakettle man.

"What is your problem?" I turned around and glared at him.

"What? No problem."

"Then, why don't you stop?"

"You should be more polite," he lectured me.

"You too could be more polite. Sssst! Sssst!" I turned away and walked on.

"Good morning," said one of the policemen, laughing.

I walked into a café, where a friendly waiter presented me with eggs, toast, sausage, and fresh coffee. Victoria Falls wasn't really so bad, I realized, and the touts were only trying to survive. I was just cranky from lack of sleep and the overnight bus ride from Namibia.

Zimbabwe was—not long ago—an African success story. In 1980, Mugabe—a war hero and intellectual—became the first democratically elected leader of the newly independent nation of Zimbabwe. Through the years, however, Mugabe's moments of brilliance became overshadowed more and more by corruption and cronyism. Land redistribution—something that much of the world agreed was necessary as land ownership had been determined by past colonial powers—turned into a violent haphazard power play that later resulted in nationwide famine and economic hyperinflation. Skilled farmers fled Zimbabwe (or were murdered), and businesses left the country. In the years that followed, international boycotts brought on a hard-currency crisis that in turn ushered in fuel shortages.

If I were to take Zimbabwe dollars out of the ATM, I'd get Zim$55 to my one U.S. dollar. But when I changed money illegally on the street, the exchange rate was Zim$250 to $300 for my single greenback. The Zimbabwe economy was doing so poorly that neighboring Zambians were walking over the bridge at the border just to do their grocery shopping. The border post was regularly closed when the mobs of people became too overwhelming.

And if lack of food and fuel didn't give touts the drive to try to convince me to buy a trinket from them, the desperation due to the HIV rate did. An average Zimbabwean could expect to live less than forty years. Many of the people trying so hard to part me from my dollars were supporting children of dead family members and neighbors.

I switched hostels after breakfast—gladly leaving the partiers and inadequate toilets behind—and then went on a horseback safari.

I had signed up for the three-hour "intermediate" ride and was the only client. As I arrived, a long line of beginners—marked by terrified grins and patient horses—was leaving the paddock.

That's odd, I thought. *Why didn't they just send me off with the beginners?*

The guide put me on a large brown horse. He mounted a white one and led me off on a private Zambezi National Park horseback safari.

We immediately came across a group of guinea fowl and three warthogs. And then we met up with my first African buffalo.

The buffalo—not normally known for his social skills and accommodating demeanor—ignored us.

To an animal, I was a horse. Sure, I was a funny-looking horse with a strange protrusion on its back, but I was a horse. Presumably, the buffalo was not an analytical thinker and it never occurred to it that a human might ride a horse.

On we went, following elephant tracks. The guide showed me how elephant tracks are as different as human fingerprints. We followed some and—not surprisingly—they led us to three elephants.

We watched the elephants for a while and then trotted on. I propped my sunglasses up on my Woolworths "one size fits all" floppy hat and rode through thorns and brambles down to the Zambezi River.

"Look, he's thinking about crossing the river." The guide pointed to an elephant on the opposite bank. A sightseeing boat pulled up. The elephant stared at the boat for a minute, appeared to decide the popping flashes were no threat, and studied the lay of the water. He walked in.

The river got deep in the middle and the elephant nearly disappeared. He swam to the other side and then reached a shallow shelf. He hauled himself up by the front legs.

"C'mon," said my guide. "I know where he's going."

We nudged our horses downriver and then stopped and waited.

Along came the elephant. He was huge—African elephants are the largest land animals in the world—and his tusks were long. I aimed my Canon.

Then the elephant saw us. His expression changed from mellow to irate, as his eyes focused directly on me. He spread his ears wide.

"He's spotted us," I said. Then, "He's running."

The elephant charged. But the horses were well ahead of him—and me. They'd known instantly that an angry elephant was chasing us and had broken into full gallops before I'd finished my sentence.

I held on tightly and looked back. I had never seen such an awesome, terrifying sight as a charging elephant with me as its quarry.

The guide was laughing, so it seemed that we weren't in any serious danger. The elephant—happy with having frightened me—turned away. We trotted a bit farther before slowing to a walk.

"Wow," I said breathlessly. "Now I know why you take novices out separately." The beginners were not taken as close to animals and certainly were not deliberately placed in front of elephants.

Then I felt for my sunglasses. They were gone.

"We'll just go and get them," said the guide. "Maybe they'll still be there. One time my hat flew away and the elephant picked it up and walked off with it."

The idea of a gigantic male African elephant twirling my gold sunglasses around with his trunk appealed to me. Nevertheless, I was glad to find them intact, at exactly the spot where we'd broken into a gallop.

We trotted back to the stable, and I was driven to town in the client transport vehicle. Adrenalin had made me too happy to be rude back to the touts and I just laughed at them. Of course, they took this as an invitation to dog my steps, so I ducked into a restaurant for an elephant-size portion of spaghetti.

A few days later—with reluctance—I joined an overland truck for a look at Botswana. The discovery of diamonds had transformed Botswana from a poor nation into a middle-income country after independence in 1966, and a stable, multiparty, almost-corruption-free government has kept it that way. Botswana can afford to be choosy about its customers, and it appears to deliberately discourage mass tourism that could damage the environment and disturb wildlife. Park entrance fees are high and access is sometimes restricted. This has resulted in well-managed national parks and sustainable conservation policies, but independent low-budget travelers had few sightseeing options available to them.

Years later, I'd work out how to see Botswana on a budget by catching public buses and trains throughout the country. But for the moment, the overland group was small and the price was right. We drove out of chaotic Zimbabwe and into diamond- and elephant-rich Botswana.

We stopped by Chobe National Park for a look at thousands of elephants before driving to the Okavango Delta. Having grown accustomed to a little independence, and not being predisposed to liking overland tours, I was champing at the bit to be on my own after about six claustrophobic minutes, and I split with the group after we went by *mokoros*—flat, wooden boats poled by locals—into the Delta. The group went camping and I caught a morning minibus south from Maun for the two-hour trip to Ghanzi.

From Ghanzi, I'd get a bus first to the Namibian border and then to Windhoek. I'd called Shawn on his cell phone to see where we could meet. We hadn't worked it out—he'd be in Swakopmund when I'd be at the border—but once I'd hung up, I'd realized that I could just go to him instead of asking him to meet me somewhere. Perhaps I had been foolish to walk away from a nice man for some nebulous possibility with Turbo, halfway across the planet. Maybe I could take this second chance, get to know Shawn without the group around, see if there was something worth pursuing between us.

When I arrived at Ghanzi, I was dismayed to see that the bus to the border was nearly empty. Buses in Africa usually don't leave until they're full, or sometimes over-full.

"Do you know when the bus leaves?" I asked a man wearing an official-looking badge.

"Maybe half past one," he said, before wandering off. That was three hours from now. I hoped he was wrong.

I asked a middle-aged woman in an enormous, traditional hoopskirt.

"Two," she said with certainty. This was even worse than the first answer.

I walked to the junction where the road to the border was. "Could I hitch?" I asked two Botswanan women at the Shell gas station for advice.

"It is not safe for a woman alone," they said firmly.

I was skeptical, but I had to bow to local advice. Deflated, I went back to wait for the bus to fill up and leave.

Four young German tourists showed up. One of them—a tall, thin man with a shaved head named Oliver—took a seat across the aisle from me. The other three—two men and a woman—spread out across the empty seats. Then a grandma squashed in next to me, sandwiching me between her and a hoopskirted woman wearing a triangular cloth hat and a small child as a lap decoration.

A Windhoek van was sitting next to us. It was empty.

"They have no license to pick you up here," explained the woman next to me. "They'll wait for you on the Namibian side of the border."

"I hope so," I said, wondering if there was any other way to Windhoek.

Finally, at two thirty, the bus was full. Actually, it was over-full and many riders stood in the aisle.

The old bus traveled slowly, stopping to pick up or drop someone off every few hundred yards. The bus is the lifeline of the community in countries where the population is mostly carless, and diamond-rich Botswana was no different from its neighbors in this respect.

The video player started. The woman next to me smiled and said, "Bruce Lee."

Huh? I looked up. It was an old Jackie Chan movie. Chan cuts across cultural boundaries. We were in for a treat.

Within no time, the bus passengers were howling with laughter. Slapstick and kung fu translate easily into any language, and every time Jackie landed a good punch or kick, the older teenage boys on the bus would yell, "Jack-*ie*!"

We started losing passengers after the movie ended and as we neared the border. Finally, no one was left on the bus except for the four Germans and me. The driver left us at the border at five thirty in the afternoon. The five-hour drive from Maun to the border post had taken nine hours.

I filled out my Botswana exit form and raced ahead of the Germans to cross the border. If there was transport, I would ask it to wait for the others.

I walked from border post to border post, across no-man's land. Then I spotted clean toilets and knew I was back in Namibia.

The immigration officer gave me some bad news.

"There's no way to get to Windhoek without hitching," he said. "But someone will give you a ride. Don't worry."

The van we'd seen back at Ghanzi was long gone, and it had probably filled up with passengers instantly from the looks of the crowd of Namibians ahead of me in the crowd of hopeful hitchers. Some of them looked as if they'd been waiting a long time.

At least we'd gained an hour. I'd gotten to Namibia at six after clearing both sides of border formalities, but we'd set our watches back and Windhoek was only three hours of paved highway away. Surely we'd find something.

I asked the first driver I saw.

"Are you going to Windhoek?"

"Sorry, I'm going the other way."

The next man I accosted had already promised his space to some of the Namibians ahead of me. When the Germans arrived, the good news was that we were at the front of the line.

We asked every driver who came through for a lift, and finally the eighth one we asked cooperated.

"I am waiting on many cars in my convoy. We can split you into different vehicles and drive you to Windhoek."

We all went to the BP gas station for dinner and a tasty meal of potato chips, jerky, and bananas. And then we waited. And waited. And waited. At eight, I desperately accosted the next man who pulled up, a Namibian man with a fuzzy beard who stepped out of an Isuzu pickup.

"I'm too tired to drive," he said. "I've been driving for three days. But I'll take the two women to Windhoek."

Actually, he said something in thickly accented English that meant approximately the same thing.

"No," we all agreed. "Not two women. One, and . . ." I pointed to Oliver. ". . . him. We're together." I had just met him eight hours ago, but I wasn't getting in the pickup truck as a single woman.

The other three Germans agreed. Oliver and I would go on ahead, and they would wait for the convoy.

It turned out that our Isuzu was part of the convoy we'd heard about earlier—the fastest part, as our driver was a speed-demon. We put our bags in the covered pickup bed and got in the cab—only to learn that we had to wait for the supervisor.

The convoy was made up of new cars and trucks, all bought at a discount in South Africa. The vehicles were being driven to Namibia for reselling at a huge profit. The supervisor brought up the rear in a little red Honda, and we had to wait for him because he had the customs paperwork and the gas money.

Finally, the paperwork was stamped. About a half dozen drivers all hung around and shot the breeze for a while.

"This man," said our driver, pointing at the supervisor, a hefty man with thick glasses and a goatee. "He is my brother. He is my white brother. He is white, and the supervisor, but I love him like my brother."

Oliver and I nodded and smiled. It was going to be a long trip.

Two of the Germans had scored a seat in another pickup, and the third was in the supervisor's car. We were all relieved when we finally got moving.

On to Windhoek!

Then, no, we were just on to the BP again for refueling.

Delivering the vehicles on empty had a financial advantage, and the supervisor had to negotiate with each driver separately to put in as little fuel as possible. The drivers didn't like to drive on empty, and each tried to negotiate for more gas.

Our driver was adamant. He wanted half a tank for the three hundred kilometers, but he got only a quarter. He shook his head as if knowing full well the quarter tank would not get him to Windhoek.

After refueling, it was time to buy junk food and chat. Oliver and I were bored at first, but that turned to concern when our driver stuck a beer in my hand.

"You want a beer. This is your beer," he prompted me.

Right. So our driver was drinking but didn't want the supervisor to know.

Oliver was wearing his seatbelt, but I was in the middle seat. There was no seatbelt. I was worried.

We left the BP at last, an hour after the first hints of departure and three hours after arriving at the border. Our driver sped ahead, just to pull over a few kilometers up the road at the East Gate BP.

"My cousin," he said, motioning at the man inside.

He went away for a minute. We waited nervously. Was this going to be another hour-long stop?

Thankfully, no. The driver had stopped only to bum two cigarettes off his cousin.

I eyeballed the East Gate Rest House, just behind the BP. "An oasis," the guidebook had called it. *Should I get off and stay the night?*

No, I decided. Windhoek was too close to give up now. We'd be there by midnight.

Off we went. The driver smoked one cigarette and then opened the beer. He guzzled it and handed the empty bottle to Oliver.

The driver motioned to the window. Oliver looked uncertain. He didn't want to throw the bottle out the window.

The driver motioned again. Oliver shrugged and tossed out the bottle. *In for a penny, in for a pound,* I thought.

There was no turning back. We'd gotten in over our heads, into madness winding down highway B6. We'd just have to keep the driver awake and sober.

Desperately we tried to engage him in conversation. Unfortunately, although we all spoke the same language, he could barely understand my accent and was hopeless with Oliver's. We both simplified our English, learning that key words or phrases could set the driver off on a rant that kept him alert and awake.

What I said:

"Is the HIV rate as high in Namibia as it is in the neighboring countries?"

What he heard:

"Blahblah HIV blah Namibia blah?"

What he said back:

"Blahblah pleaseJesusblah . . . I have one wife . . . blah . . . HIV . . . danger . . . one wife . . . my children need me . . . blahblahblah different now . . . one wife . . . HIV. . . blah . . . Jesus."

We were communicating, sort of.

"A Chinese man in Zambia," he said. "Found . . ." He struggled for the words.

"Important research," I suggested. "Possible breakthrough."

He nodded. "I pray to Jesus."

Continued conversation indicated that he had fourteen children, and one of them was either born today or had a birthday today. He also told us that the roads were dangerous at night, because kudu tended to wander onto the highway (thus the phrase "crazy kudu").

When conversation became too taxing, Oliver and I would give up. Then we'd notice the driver nodding off, and one of us would engage him again.

"You are sleepy?" I asked.

"Yes."

"I can drive." I pointed to myself and mimicked driving.

"Woman? Driving me?" He howled with laughter at such a ridiculous thought.

He asked where we'd come from.

"Okavango Delta. Chobe. Victoria Falls."

The mention of Vic Falls sent him on an anti-Mugabe rant.

"Mugabe is bad. The white man is my brother. I do not need to kill him to get his land."

While this was perhaps an oversimplification of Zimbabwe's problems, it was well said.

We went 120 kilometers per hour all the way to Gobabis, arriving there at ten after an hour of driving. We waited at the gas station. We were running on empty and needed the supervisor to pay for fuel.

But the supervisor was going eighty kilometers per hour and bringing up the rear. We waited. The German couple arrived and joined us in our wait.

"This is excruciating," said one. "It's such a short distance, but it is taking forever."

I looked in my guidebook again. Gobabis had two decent hotels and frequent daytime connections to Windhoek.

Then our driver had an idea.

"Seventy dollars of petrol," he announced.

Oliver and I pooled our money and put US$8.50 worth of gas into the tank. If we could go before the others showed up, we'd be in Windhoek in two hours.

The gas went in, and we were off. We'd driven out of the gas station and into the street when the supervisor pulled in.

Our driver stopped and got out.

"Shit," I said. Oliver nodded agreement.

Half an hour later, our driver had been reimbursed (meaning that we had paid him for the lift) and shot the breeze with his supervisor-brother. Blatantly lying, Oliver and I had both assured the supervisor that our driver never went above eighty—we couldn't imagine why our Isuzu used so much gas.

Finally, I went to the driver. Obviously, getting angry would not help. But perhaps stern instructions would.

"C'mon," I said, as if I were a schoolteacher speaking to a naughty child. "Let's go."

He followed docilely and we left Gobabis.

"They tell me that I am too tired, that I must stay in Gobabis and sleep. Never. My son was born today." He looked disgusted, and then he drove on the right side of the road for a while.

Namibians, like all Southern Africans, drive on the left. Our driving on the right did not fill me with confidence.

Then our driver began swerving all over. I hoped a kudu, or another car, didn't come around the bend.

He couldn't keep his eyes open. I nudged Oliver—what could we do? Beg to be let out in the middle of the desert? I stared hard at the Southern Cross, wondering if this was it. *Had I finally pushed it too far? How lucky would we be tonight, and what would it feel like to be in a car crash at such a high speed?* The stars made me think of Turbo, waiting for me in Australia. He would not be pleased that I'd flirted with Shawn. He'd be even less pleased if I died in an auto accident in Namibia.

Then, after I contemplated my seemingly impending doom for what seemed like hours but could have been only one, the driver pulled over and stopped.

"Please," he whispered to Oliver. "Help me."

Oliver was delighted to oblige. The two changed places and the driver instantly fell into a deep sleep.

Oliver fastened his seatbelt and sped up to 120. But he was a good driver, and he was used to driving on the left as he had been working in South Africa for several months, selling interior design products.

I would've been happy to go to sleep myself, but I couldn't abandon Oliver. I was in a waking-dream state, asking disconnected questions just to keep talking.

"Do you like interior design? Do you think it's easy to drive on the left?"

But there was no danger of Oliver's falling asleep. The only danger was from kudus and other animals that might wander into our path.

The last three hours of the long journey passed quickly as I dozed and then shook myself awake. We got to the police checkpoint on the outskirts of Windhoek.

"How are we going to explain this?" I asked.

"They'll just let us go. Buckle his seatbelt," said Oliver. I struggled to belt in my neighbor, who didn't wake up.

The police smiled and waved us on.

We drove in, to Sam Nujoma Drive.

"I know where we are," said Oliver. He was also on his second trip to Namibia.

Oliver drove us straight to the Cardboard Box. We were able to get our bags out of the truck—the pickup bay wasn't locked. It was after one in the morning.

"Wake up, wake up!" Oliver shook the driver. "We are in Windhoek!"

The driver woke up, shook our hands, and got behind the

wheel. His eyelids were heavy and he didn't appear to understand. Nevertheless, he started the engine and slowly drove away.

Ephraim, the driver and security guard of the Cardboard Box, was awake and let us in.

The dorms were locked, with people asleep inside. We'd have to sleep in the TV room for the night.

"I'd be happy to," I said. "I'll sleep anywhere. I'm just glad to be alive."

The TV room was as comfortable as a dorm, anyway. I slept soundly on the shag carpet, next to this German interior designer I barely knew but with whom I had shared a life-and-death experience

The next morning, the Cardboard Box travel agent gave me some bad news.

"It's a holiday weekend. There's nowhere to stay in Swakopmund."

So my planned quad-biking excursion was off. But Shawn would be along shortly. His tent was still up in the backyard. I'd just wait for him. I looked out of the big bay window in the common room.

The Isuzu was still outside. The driver had made it no farther than across the road before parking and going to sleep.

I found Oliver. Together we approached the pickup.

"Should we wake him?" wondered Oliver.

"It is nine o'clock, and he was anxious to get home last night."

Oliver tapped on the window. The driver moved. He waved us away.

We went back into the Cardboard Box, but about ten minutes later, I spotted the driver out of his truck, talking to Ephraim.

We went back out. The driver looked happy to see us and shook Oliver's hand.

"You were really tired," we explained. "You've slept all night. Shouldn't you go home now, or maybe you should call your squad?"

This question reminded him that he was on the job.

"My squad," he said slowly. "Where is my squad?"

We shrugged. Considering his state the night before, he was lucky to be alive. We hadn't thought to find his squad for him, as we couldn't even wake him up.

Oliver and I retreated in haste before the driver could get any more anxious. We looked again an hour later—he was gone.

I splurged on my own room for two nights. I did my laundry and enjoyed fast Internet connections, good restaurants, and well-stocked grocery stores. I chatted with Oliver a few times, but we were both suddenly bashful in the daylight, as if now that our shared experience was over, we had no idea what to say to each other. I sat in front of the picture window in the Cardboard Box common area. Every time someone came into the yard, I'd look up to see if it was Shawn.

But unknown to me, Shawn had taken a group to climb Spitzkoppe mountain, hurt his back, and ended up spending the weekend in physical therapy at Swakopmund State Hospital. Fate had intervened. My loyalty to Turbo and my skittish paranoia about relationships was intact by default.

Chapter 4

I'd Turn Back if I Were You

I hadn't expected to love Africa, and it caught me by surprise. Africa had just been a place on my "to do" list.

> *To Do:*
> *Wash clothes*
> *Buy toilet paper*
> *See Africa*

An African safari was an obligatory adventure for the hardcore traveler. Like visiting Antarctica or Papua New Guinea, a trip to Africa separated the casual vacationer from the truly dedicated. I'd added the Cape Town-to-Cairo leg to MariesWorldTour.com primarily because it seemed obligatory.

But the open savannas, wildlife, and easy atmosphere of Southern Africa had caught me off guard and charmed me. And while I wasn't fond of the massive overland-truck scene, the more intimate backpacker's network—something I'd shunned in the crowded hostels of Southeast Asia and Australia—was small enough to be appealing.

Disappointed by Shawn's vanishing act and unaware of his stay in the Swakopmund State Hospital, I'd angrily written him off and caught the bus from Windhoek back to Vic Falls, this time being pulled over in the middle of the night to be counted by Namibian census-takers. I'd navigated the touts on the Zimbabwe side with learned humor before heading to Kariba to join a canoe safari.

"There are four things to watch out for on the Zambezi," announced Bono, the tall, healthy-looking river guide on my four-day Shearwater Canoe Safari, at the launch site. "One: crocs. Don't stick your hands or feet in the water. Two: hippos. They have four-inch teeth. Let them know you're here like this." He tapped his paddle loudly on the canoe. "Three: visible tree stumps. Avoid them. Four: tree stumps below the surface. You can identify them by the way the water flows on the surface. Okay?"

Uh, sure. Tree stumps didn't worry me. As a single traveler, I was partnered with Bono. Crocs didn't worry me either—I had no plans to drape my limbs into the water.

But hippos, some of the very animals I'd come to see, worried me. The most dangerous animals in Africa are vegetarian, but they'll still bite you if you're between them and the safety of deep water.

A few hours later, I was too tired to be worried. I was rowing in the front—the person in the back of a canoe does 80 percent of the work—but I was still clumsy, sweating, and wondering why I hadn't realized that a canoe safari would involve physical exertion. The sun beat down and a wind blew against us. Our line of four two-person canoes hugged the Zimbabwean shore just north of the put-in point at Chirundu. The Zambian shore was visible on the other side of deep water, which we avoided to minimize our risk of an unexpected hippo encounter.

I thought this was supposed to be fun, I thought, before wondering—to my great embarrassment—if I could leave early and hitch a ride back to Kariba.

After a brief stop for pink-lunch-meat-and-cucumber sand-wiches, I weakly rowed to a flat, sandy area surrounded by African scrub, our campsite for the night. We were on a small island next to Zimbabwe's Hurungwe Safari Area and would approach the Mana Pools National Park shoreline tomorrow. Zambia's coast was rural but inhabited—we wouldn't glimpse Zambia's Lower Zambezi National Park until our final day.

Bono smiled his all-knowing benevolent-drill-sergeant smile and then issued some more instructions.

"After dark," he said, "don't go anywhere near the riverbank. That's where the crocodiles hunt. And at night, if you need a toilet, don't go more than ten meters from your tent."

This was a bit alarming, as I'd just been considering sneaking down to the shore to wash. Fortunately, the "bucket behind a tree" method was available.

We set up our two-person tents while Bono and the junior guide,

Cambell, made us a camp dinner of rice, chicken stew, and African gem squash. Everyone was exhausted and we all were resting on our sleeping mats by nine in spite of the possible presence of man-eating wild animals.

I shared a tent with Sara, a thirty-one-year-old volunteer teacher from the United Kingdom. She'd been in the countryside for two years—teaching Zimbabwean businesspeople how to make business plans—but she had little faith in her effectiveness.

"They're developing good business plans," she explained. "But there's no money to be had. There just isn't any funding."

In the morning, the wind was with us. Canoeing was easier, although my fingers and palms were tender. I'd obviously been gripping the paddle too hard. But I relaxed as I realized I'd gotten the hang of it. I no longer had to struggle and was not dripping water all over the canoe with each stroke.

About a half hour after pushing off, we encountered a huge pod of dozens of hippos that stretched from Zimbabwe to Zambia across the Zambezi's narrow width. I was in the lead boat with Bono, and I had thought this advantageous, as Bono was the man carrying the loaded warning pistol. Now, as he carefully led the group through the hippo pool, I realized that being the first to potentially surprise a hippopotamus was rather risky.

To intimidate us or perhaps to let us know to avoid them, the hippos emitted ominous roars that sounded like the disembodied Jolly Green Giant.

"Ho, ho, ho," bellowed the hippos.

"I'd turn back if I were you." That's what they're saying, I thought.

Bono slowly paddled us into the middle of the pod. He kept tapping his oar against the canoe to let the hippos know we were coming.

"Stay close," he said to the rest of the group.

Hippos exploded out of the water around us. They can stay under water for five to six minutes and when they come up suddenly, the result is a massive expulsion of air and water followed by a surprised pair of eyes and a pinkish snout.

I was wondering if Bono had been lying to me about a legendary hippo that could bite a canoe in half, when he started issuing instructions.

"Follow me," he barked. He'd been aiming right for a hippo and now suddenly cut directly across the river into deep water.

"Paddle left," he told me. I paddled furiously on the left. Sweat and effort didn't bother me anymore. If we didn't make it in time, I'd be the first one bitten by the unhappy hippopotamus.

We made it in spite of my feeble contribution. Now I understood the appeal of the Lower Zambezi canoe safari. We were face-to-face with nature, without the filter of a car window.

I quit pretending my paddling mattered and enthusiastically took as many photos as I did strokes for the rest of the journey. We were ahead of schedule, and Bono instructed us to slow down.

Slow down we did, observing more hippos, some devilish-looking crocs, elephants, egrets, and carmine bee-eater birds that lived in holes along the muddy riverbank.

Late on the third morning, we paddled to the bank to indulge in more pink-lunch-meat-and-cucumber treats. Afterward, everyone else wandered off and left me sitting on a sleeping mat, scribbling in my diary.

Then they all came scampering back, wide-eyed and agitated. "Elephants."

Bono had the warning pistol in his hand, and Cambell had the two-way radio. It was on.

"If an elephant charges," instructed Bono. "Stand still."

Was he out of his mind? But there was no time to argue.

The elephants—seven of them—approached. The day was hot, and they headed straight toward the river's edge—and our canoes— for drinks and showers.

The elephants inadvertently herded us.

"Everyone over here," said Bono, motioning us farther on, out of the elephants' path.

The elephants stared at us as we quaked. They seemed to decide we were not worth their time. They trundled on, to drink and splash about while we cowered and snapped once-in-a-lifetime photos.

The elephants finally wandered off after about twenty minutes of splashing around. High on adrenalin, we reclaimed our canoes.

But our encounter wasn't over. Five more elephants approached, shaking the berries off acacia trees as they walked. This time they approached directly, driving us up onto the bank. We were cornered, our only potential escape a leap into the croc-infested river. But the elephants didn't care about us. They had eyes only for the cooling effects of water, squirted onto their backs by their swaying trunks.

The most amazing thing about the African elephant is not the size of its enormous ears, which flap to provide elephant air-conditioning. It is its sensitive, delicate step. They avoided our canoes and possessions and even the camp doo-doo shovel without so much as a glance.

They left the water's edge at last and moved away, intent on tormenting more acacia trees.

Buffalos wandered up next, along with waterbucks.

"Still want to go on that game walk?" joked Bono. We'd been pestering him for a game walk, but he'd refused because walking in the national park was strictly controlled.

Nobody wanted to go. Why go for a game walk when the game will come to you?

We paddled another four miles.

"Hey," yelled a man from the bank in midafternoon. He was fishing with his son. "Is this where that croc killed that man last year?"

"No," said Bono. "It was back there." He pointed behind us.

"Um, Bono," I asked nervously, "are we camping around here?"

"Yes," he answered.

We pulled up shortly and set up camp on a sandy island. I washed from a bucket and then asked Bono if I could leave my towel out to dry. In Kariba, local advice had been to take wet laundry inside otherwise the baboons were likely to steal my underwear.

"No, don't leave it out," he said. "The Zambians might take it."

I stared at him, uncertain if he were joking. I decided to risk it.

The stars were out in force, and the Milky Way was clear. We stared at the sky for a while, and then Sara and I went back to our tent. We talked about Zimbabwe.

"It's an amazing country," I said. I meant it. I had come a long way from despising Vic Falls, and I meant what I was saying. "What a shame that things are going to hell."

"Yeah," she agreed. "My agency is pulling out. They're expecting food shortages, because so many crops failed or were burned. And the people here are so peaceful—they hate fighting. I hope our guides have an escape plan."

I told her that I'd had dinner with two of Zimbabwe's thirty thousand white citizens back in Kariba.

"Zimbabwe's fantastic," one had said to me. "I couldn't live anywhere else."

"If everything falls apart here," said the other, "I'll be the last one here to turn the lights off."

On that note, we tried to sleep. It didn't really work out, though. Elephants splashed nearby, vocal hippos gathered and socialized, ducks quacked, and lions on the mainland roared all night.

I left my towel out. No Zambians took it.

Chapter 5

East Africa Express

I slept uneasily in my hostel bed, certain that I wouldn't wake up on time and would miss the bus to the southern terminus of the Tanzania-Zambia Railway. At three, I dreamed that I looked at my watch and it read five. I was in the worn-out but warmhearted Chachacha Backpackers' dorm in Lusaka, Zambia, and I didn't want to wake up the Peace Corps volunteers sleeping around me. I quietly dragged my bag out into the hall so I could dress and pack in the bathroom. Only when I got into the bathroom and turned on the light did I look at my watch, wide-awake this time, and realize my mistake.

I tried again a few hours later and this time got it right. The

Lusaka municipal water supply was still off—having been cut the night before ten minutes after I'd showered (no correlation between these events, I hoped)—but someone had left a pot of water on a burner in the outside kitchen used by backyard campers. I boiled it and treated myself to a breakfast of coffee and instant oatmeal.

Water and power frequently go off in certain African cities. Sometimes this is by accident, but often it is by design, intended to control conservation of resources in areas where the population has outgrown the infrastructure. The good news was that the tap water (when it was on) was drinkable in almost every place I'd visited so far. Everyone on the canoe safari had been reduced to drinking the water that came straight out of the tap at Kariba Breezes Hotel, and no one had gotten ill from it.

A black cat scampered across my path as I left Chachacha Back-packers. I contemplated it, wondering about superstition, and because I was studying the cat intently I did not notice an upcoming rock and nearly sprained my ankle. *Proof,* I thought, *that the adage is true.*

I'd just gotten off the bus from the Zimbabwe border last night, and here I was planning to get on another bus to find my way north to Tanzania. I'd expected Shearwater Canoe Safaris to drop me by the side of the road yesterday, leaving me to hitch to the border while the outfitters took our group back to Kariba. But the Shearwater driver had kindly left the group lunching by the side of the road and driven Bono and me to the border. Once there, Bono pointed me in the right direction.

"That's the border post." He pointed at a short concrete building that was surrounded by a huge mob of people who had just gotten off a bus from Harare.

Great.

It would have been so easy to just walk across the border without going into the building full of bureaucrats. But I needed to get a stamp into Zambia, or I'd be fined on the way out tomorrow night. I lined up behind fifty others, a little embarrassed that I'd even consider crossing illegally just to avoid a queue.

The wait was interminable, made longer by standing, baking in the sun. Finally, barely squeezing my forty-pound pack through the door, I edged my way into the building. Being out of the sun was a relief, but the line still snaked around inside. A half hour went by as I shuffled forward. The smack of stamps being imprinted on passports every few minutes reassured me that the line was still moving. I was hungry and thought enviously of the lunch of processed meat that the canoe group had been eating as I'd left them. Too bad I hadn't thought to grab a slice of bread.

I finally reached the counter, just as the clerk left for lunch. I felt a moment of panic as I realized I could be standing here for another half hour. I called to him.

"Please," I said. "Just stamp me out of Zimbabwe. I've been waiting a long time."

He glared at me and at the dozens of people behind me. I placed my passport on the counter and smiled brightly. Finally, he stamped it and slid it back to me before leaving. He didn't smile back at my foolish grin, but that didn't matter. I had my exit visa.

I skulked out without looking back, guiltily knowing that while my plea had worked (barely), everyone else behind me would have to continue to wait.

I trudged and sweated my way across the bridge over the Zambezi, through no-man's land into Zambia. I felt the rush of exhilaration, even though I'd been in Zambia only a week earlier when I'd gone to Lusaka to book my TAZARA train ticket. Border posts are mundane places—existing for the processing of paperwork—but they are frontiers and still represent the possibility of something new and exciting.

The thrill was lost a few minutes later. I was pleased to find that the Zambian border office had air-conditioning, but the fifty-passenger bus from Harare had arrived ahead of me once again. It took me a long time to get to the front of the line before emerging victorious into Zambia, and then I had to wait an additional forty minutes to be waved through a gate—where I boarded a cramped minibus with fifteen adults, two children, and a lot of luggage for the short ride to Lusaka. My pack was jammed under a seat, and someone's box had been placed directly beneath my feet. One of the children stared at me with wide eyes. My aching knees reminded me that I don't have the joints for this kind of travel, but fortunately the drive was only two hours long. I arrived sweating and dusty in Lusaka and headed straight to the shower at Chachacha Backpackers.

This morning's bus to Kapiri Moshi was a full-size coach, complete with video screens, curtains, and air-conditioning. We were due to leave at seven, but the bus sold out and left fifteen minutes early. I was surprised to see a blond head rising above a headrest a few rows in front of me.

Sappy ballads about Jesus blasted out of the bus loudspeakers. The paved road was smooth, and after an hour, the ballad tape was turned off and *Twins* came on the video monitor.

We stopped in Kapiri Moshi at nine—missing the reunion of Arnold Schwarzenegger, Danny DeVito, and mother—and only three of us disembarked, while the other passengers continued to the town center.

"Do you know where the train station is?" asked Vicki, the blond I'd spotted who turned out to be a thirty-one-year-old British development worker.

"No. Do you?" I addressed her Zambian boyfriend, Mubiana.

He laughed his charming, honest laugh that hid no cynicism. I'd hear it a lot during the next week. Mubiana's ethnicity gave him credibility that my obvious foreignness did not give me, but it made him no better informed than I was. It was his first time here too. Vicki and Mubiana lived in the western part of Zambia, where he directed a church choir and she worked with her British development service.

The guy who had sat next to me on the bus had instructed me to walk north along the road for one kilometer and then turn right to reach the train, so the three of us did that, to the accompaniment of children screaming "howareyou howareyou" from their front yards.

"I get this every day," said Vicki. Even the youngest Zambian children learn the phrase "how are you" in school and are eager to practice it. Vicki laughed off the screaming children while explaining that she had tried to buy two first-class tickets for the train ride, but they'd been sold out. I was glad I'd made the special trip to Lusaka and booked with TAZARA last week.

My relief was short-lived. We found the TAZARA station, but the man at the ticket office had no record of my booking. He directed me to "Customer Service," where a Zambian woman in her thirties with a pale cataract over her left pupil was slowly recording every passenger's occupation in a ledger.

"Wait here," she said. She wandered off, returning ten minutes later with a list of second-class bookings.

"Your name is not on here," she said.

"*First* class," I repeated. "I booked first class." The compartments were similar, but first class had four berths while second class had six per compartment. And first-class passengers, it was rumored, had access to a lounge.

"You booked first class?" She parroted my words back to me. "Wait a minute."

She wandered off again, returning with the first-class list.

"You're not on here, either," she said with satisfaction.

"Yes, well, I booked last week at the TAZARA office in Lusaka. I confirmed on Monday with an international call from Zimbabwe."

She didn't care. "Go see the chief booking clerk."

I dragged my bag around back and sat on it, in front of the empty and locked office of the chief booking clerk. He showed up ten minutes later and explained.

"We had to give all the first-class compartments to the ministers," he said.

Ah, so that was it. Some important officials had come along, bumping all the nonofficials out. My efforts at booking had been for nothing, and I was ticketless.

"Please forgive us," said the chief booking clerk. "We can sell you a second-class ticket."

I resigned myself to another long train ride in a yearlong series of hellish train rides. The worst had been through Central Asia, where the conductor had used my phrasebook and some creative body language to ask me for sex. No matter how long the trip to Tanzania, it couldn't be as bad as that.

I bought a newspaper and a box of Chips Ahoy! from a newsstand and ate myself into a sugar-induced stupor. My mood changed for the better when I read that Zambians insult people by calling each other "cabbage."

At noon, the third-class stampede began. Seats were first-come, first-served, and everyone desperately wanted the most tolerable seat for the 1,150-mile journey.

Uniformed railroad officials bodily stopped the crowd, letting through twenty at a time and then bravely throwing themselves in front of the mob as human barriers. Women with tightly packed bundles on their heads and babies strapped to their backs pulled toddlers along while jockeying for position, while men used suitcases to carve out personal space. The passengers were dressed in both Western clothes and African prints. Of the women, only Vicki and I wore trousers. All other women wore skirts—some Western, others colorful and locally tailored—as is common outside of cities north of the Zambezi. In urban areas, younger women often wear jeans with wide belts and baby T-shirts, just like their contemporaries in North America or Europe.

Those of us with assigned seats watched the chaos, and when the crowd thinned, the first and second class boarded.

I was in Car 5, which resembled—and probably *was*—an ancient Chinese six-berth "hard sleeper" (since the Chinese had built the TAZARA railway in the 1970s). The condition of the car was rickety, and the upper berths are raised during the day so all six passengers must sit on the lower two berths all day long. Add everyone's groceries and food routines to the mix, and the bottom two berths of a six-berth sleeper become a crumb-covered, disorganized mess.

The others in my compartment were quiet and sweet—two Zambian women and one Kenyan. The TAZARA compartments are gender-segregated—a real relief to me after the ride through Central Asia. I still wanted a first-class berth, so that I could use the lounge. I found the attendant.

"Hello. How are you? I was wondering if there might be any first-class berths available?" I tried smiling. It had worked at the border.

"I am sorry, madam." Everyone in Zambia seemed to call me madam. "The ministers have taken all the first-class berths."

Oh. Nevertheless, I walked through the line of cars until I found the lounge. How was anyone to know I didn't have a first-class ticket? I marched to the front counter.

"What time does the movie start? And what is the movie?"

The attendant did not ask for my ticket or tell me the name of the movie. Instead he just told me the movie showing times before waving me in.

At dinnertime, I walked back toward my compartment, but Vicki and Mubiana stopped me along the way. They had spoken to the conductor at the right moment and gotten upgraded. They were sharing with a Marinko and Sebastian, a pair of twentysomethings from Central Europe. Apparently, men and women tourists could share compartments as long as all agreed to it, since it is widely assumed that foreign tourists are rather odd (and improper) to begin with. Marinko—who felt sorry for me—made it his personal crusade to get me an upgrade. He was a polite and attractive young European, well dressed in his new travel gear, and like his blond travel companion, he had a smile for everyone.

Marinko tracked down the conductor and bullied him into allowing me to move. The ministers—invisible to begin with—mysteriously evaporated and I was given a top bunk in a room with three Zambian women, right next door to my new friends.

The four-berth first-class compartments were nicer than the second-class compartments, but the biggest benefit to first-class carriages on any train is that the toilets—which emptied straight onto the tracks—host a third fewer people.

I had a chicken and rice dinner in the dining car before being lulled to sleep by the loud, constant chatting of the woman in the berth below mine. I woke only to show my passport to a Zambian border guard in the middle of the night.

It was not quite seven when the chatting began again.

I opened my eyes. Across from me was a plump Zambian woman

sleeping in peach satin pajamas and wearing a hairnet. I closed my eyes again, but the chattering from below was incessant. An important discussion on the merits of face cream seemed imminent. I tried to ignore it. I had no reasons to get out of bed early, no pressing engagements on this long train ride to Dar Es Salaam.

The talk of face cream woke and then engaged the other three residents of the car. The Zambian women rose and removed their hairnets. Their morning routine was totally different from the morning train routines I'd seen elsewhere in the world. Everywhere else I'd been, people wore the same clothes day after day and just got dirtier and dirtier, unless there happened to be a shower on the train.

Here, the women clearly did not consider a lack of running water to be an excuse for poor hygiene. They stripped, slathered various creams onto their bodies, and then opened their suitcases to reveal perfectly pressed outfits. Each one applied makeup meticulously. This was done at a methodical, unhurried pace, and so I waited on my top bunk. These were not poor women, and while the urban female train attendants were all thin, fat is a sign of wealth in rural Zambia. There was not room for a fourth person to stand in the compartment.

One woman slid open the door. A man was right outside, picking his nose en route to the toilets. His head turned at the sound of the door and he looked in.

The chatterer stood naked from the waist up. She calmly crossed her arms over her naked breasts and stood proudly without any sign of alarm. The man walked on, showing no indication of embarrassment. The door slid shut. Everyone in the compartment looked at me and giggled.

"In your culture," said the chatterer to me, "the breasts are private."

"Yes," I agreed.

"In our culture," she explained, "the breasts are not such a big deal, but here is very private."

She motioned to her thighs.

I laughed. "Where I come from, that's private too."

The women all looked at me with apparent skepticism. Maybe they'd seen too many popular movies that suggested otherwise.

We crossed into Tanzania at ten thirty. Only another day and a half to sit on the train.

The day was long and slow, a dreamlike state of boredom broken up by meals in the dining car and walks to and from the lounge. I'd visit Vicki and Mubiana and then pace to the lounge again until the bad action movies forced me out. I chased getting hot water for instant soup for about three hours until finally a waiter told me it simply could not be done because the burners in the kitchen were being used.

Our train lurched on into the night. We'd stop (frequently), wait for a while, and then the train would jerk spastically and lurch forward.

I went to the lounge to watch the evening film. Maybe it would make the next hour and a half pass by quickly.

"What's the movie?" I asked the attendant.

"I don't know," he said, looking at the video screen. "Schwarzenegger."

"Obviously," I muttered. I had passed the point where enthusiasm could curb grumpiness, where dullness could be tempered by the exhilaration of knowing I was on a train in the middle of Africa. If the video was so indistinguishable that even a man who had seen it a dozen times could not identify it, why would I bother?

I went back to my berth. Maybe I could sleep long enough that the trip would be over when I next opened my eyes.

That plan didn't work. The next time I opened my eyes, I was still on the TAZARA train, on the top bunk in a first-class compartment. The sun streamed in through the slats covering the window, indicating that we'd all managed to sleep past seven this time.

My Zambian lady-friends' good spirits were also flagging. They still went through their morning rituals—though the car was beginning to take on the faint smell of body odor under the lotions they rubbed in—but they did them an hour later than they had the day before. I could guess what they must be thinking—that the later they slept, the less time they'd have to look at this damn train. Their morning greetings were briefer and less indulgent. Communications became limited to grunts and essential words. "Open." "Shut." "Borrow cream."

Suffering from excessive boredom, I went to the lounge car and ordered a bottle of Coke. I sat by the window, drank it slowly, and watched Tanzania go by. *If only*, I thought, *I'd gotten to Lusaka earlier so that I could have gone to the bookstore. If only I had beaten the Harare busload of people to the Zimbabwe border. If only I'd taken a bus from Lusaka to Dar Es Salaam.* Buses are faster than trains in Africa. Why hadn't I taken a bus? Had I really believed the train would be so much more comfortable and exotic? *Next time,* I thought—*if there is a next time—next time I'll take a bus.*

We'd entered Tanzania from the southwest and were steadily plowing north and east toward the central coast. The number of trees seemed to increase, and the foliage thickened. Crowds would appear out of the bush and congregate around the train when it stopped. Tanzanian villagers would stare in at us and we'd stare out at them.

The train entered Selous Game Reserve, and I joined my neighbors for their first looks at wild African animals. Mubiana, in spite of living his entire life in Zambia, had never encountered a giraffe. His eyes lit up when the train scared dozens of them, sending them galloping for the safety of the nearest cover.

Sebastian and Marinko, meanwhile, had not been on a safari yet and were practically hopping up and down with excitement.

Mubiana was the best spotter, but being a quiet man, he'd just point when he saw an animal. Marinko and Sebastian would follow Mubiana's motion and yell out "zebra" or "giraffe." Then we'd all hang out of the window.

Selous Game Reserve, at four times the size of Serengeti, is the largest game reserve in Africa. But only the northern end, which the TAZARA train skirts, hosts safaris. Thousands of animals live in the reserve, but they are spread out. Some say the best way to get into the park is from the air. Selous is not unique among African game parks aside from one point. It has about thirteen hundred wild dogs, a species that is nearly extinct in other places and that remains my personal "holy grail" of safari animals. But wild dogs are shy and don't approach trains. We didn't see any wild dogs from our window.

Selous is only four hours from Dar Es Salaam, but we were already running late before we ever entered the park. Our trip from Kapiri Moshi, Zambia, clocked in at fifty-three hours by the time we all stepped, dizzy and stinking, onto the platform in Dar Es Salaam, Tanzania.

Chapter 6

Zanzibar Gloom

On the island of Zanzibar, a tout dogged my steps for the quarter-mile walk from the ferry port to my hotel.

"Jambo," he said, the Swahili word for "hello" but used in tourist areas as an opening greeting to a sales pitch. "I can help you find a hotel."

"Listen," I replied. "I already have a reservation, so you're wasting your time. You're not getting a commission for a prebooked room."

"You might get lost."

"I have a map."

He continued to follow me.

"Look at all those other tourists." I pointed back to the ferry port. "They don't have hotels. What is the point in following me? Go make money!" It hadn't occurred to me before that the advent of Internet bookings would affect the lives of touts.

He persistently followed me all the way to Emerson and Green Hotel. Once dubbed "one of the best small hotels" by a London newspaper, it was an atmospheric old merchant's mansion with individually decorated suites. It was a splurge for me, even though I'd cheekily asked for a discount and taken the smallest room—one on the second-floor interior courtyard that still included solid wooden double doors and traditional local antique furniture despite being the hotel's cheapest room. When I'd booked it months ago, I'd reasoned that I would need a rest midway through Africa. What better place than Zanzibar, famed for its beaches, spices, ancient town, and Arabic flavor?

The tout stayed a few steps behind me as I tried to discourage him, first by walking quickly, then by reasoning with him, and then by walking slowly. I found the hotel with the aid of my map and checked in, while the tout hung around the lobby, perhaps hoping someone would tip him to go away. I dumped my dusty backpack into my upscale room and then went for a walk. Maybe I could find Vicki and Mubiana. They'd left Dar Es Salaam for Zanzibar a day ahead of me. Marinko and Sebastian had gone on to Arusha to go on a safari to Serengeti National Park.

The tiny alleys of Zanzibar's main town—Stone Town— reminded me of similar ones I'd seen in Damascus and Jerusalem. Barely three people could walk side by side, but that didn't stop motorbikes, wheelbarrows, and bicycles from using the narrow walkways. The mazelike paths lay in no discernible pattern, having been established up to three hundred years ago when urban planning was not a top priority. Most of the ground-level dwellings were storefronts, many of them selling souvenirs and tours. Stone Town is renowned for its Arabic flavor, having once been a major trading post for both spices and African slaves. Minarets dot the landscape, as Zanzibar is populated almost entirely by Muslims.

I stopped at an Internet café to check my mail before checking out Zanzibar's excursions. *Maybe I should have a look at one of these famous beaches,* I thought. *Or maybe I should just enjoy my gorgeous hotel room. Or wander the streets listening to the call to prayer while sidestepping cracks in the alleys.* I was lost in thought and anticipation as I walked out of the computer alcove and into the main lobby to pay for my computer time.

High on the wall, a television was turned on, with the CNN logo showing across the bottom of the screen. Two familiar buildings were on the screen.

They were on fire.

My question was rhetorical, really. I knew damn well which buildings these were. I'd commuted through them, shopped in them, and bought half-price Broadway theater tickets in them. I spoke my question aloud—shakily, not because I needed an answer, but because I needed confirmation that I wasn't watching a bad action movie.

"Is that the World Trade Center?"

The two teens who worked at the Internet café nodded and giggled. They thought it was funny that two giant skyscrapers were on fire.

"Planes hit them," one boy said with apparent delight, and then he noticed my expression. "What's wrong?" I had probably gone pale. "Those are office buildings," I said. "Lots of people work there."

The kids quit giggling.

"How many?"

"Thousands," I replied. *"Thousands."*

We all stared at CNN. There was no more laughter.

Other tourists stopped as they left or entered the computer room. The Arabic owner of the shop came out of his office and stood with us. We all stared, mostly in silence, but occasionally someone would rattle on nervously, talking too much or too loudly. Sometimes, that someone was me. Tears welled in my eyes as Mayor Giuliani—at whom I'd chafed for his aggressive anticrime measures, especially when his administration had sent a tank named "Sunny" onto my East Village street during squatter evictions—spoke of people jumping out of World Trade Center windows.

Of course, we'd seen nothing yet. The Pentagon was hit too, and false reports had us believing that fires and car bombs were going off all over northwest D.C.

At home, my friend Yancey and his dog watched live from a Jersey City pier on the Hudson River as the twin towers collapsed, their steel frames buckling from heat generated by jet-fuel fireballs.

"I've never seen anything more horrifying," emailed Yancey.

Other friends saw it from their rooftops, and they watched soot-covered business people trudging northward throughout the day. My entire neighborhood was closed down, and traffic couldn't get in or out for days, although restaurants reportedly stayed open. Friends reported women's high-heeled shoes lying on Broadway, deserted by fleeing owners. My financial adviser had been standing near the towers, having just come out of the subway. He fled blindly through the debris until he felt a door, which opened. He ran with hundreds of others down into the ground, climbing stairs lower and lower into the bowels of a nearby building.

I knew none of this at the time . . . all I knew was that for the first time, my mother sent me a note that she was happy I was in Africa instead of home in Manhattan.

People from all over the world stared at CNN with me, shook their heads, and grieved over the loss of innocent lives. Local Muslims were as distressed as tourists. There was no anti-American sentiment this day—that came later—for the moment, nationalities were forgotten and we were all simply human.

Eventually, no one was crying anymore, and people were joking nervously—in the way that people do when they don't know how to behave.

CNN's live broadcasts took on a cinema-esque quality, and I adjusted slowly to the idea that a new world order was a possibility the next time I got out of bed. *Was World War III on the way?* There was no way to know. I emailed some plans to my mother, assuming there was no point in going home, and all commercial planes were grounded anyway. I'd continue with my trip if no bombs were dropped. I'd head south to Cape Town if Sudan and Egypt started looking dicey, and from there I would search for a ship to Australia if getting home proved unwise or difficult. If there were no ships, I'd go rent an apartment in Swakopmund until things stabilized.

My quaint hotel room had no TV, and I couldn't tear myself away from the news so I spent all day at the Internet café. Finally, at ten o'clock that night, the Internet place closed. I moved next door to a hotel lobby and watched silently with a group of tourists and Africans, but CNN was just repeating itself. What was left to say? I walked back toward Emerson and Green.

"Jambo," said a dreadlocked man in a suit, hurrying to keeping pace with me in the dark street.

"Hello," I said, quickening. He kept up.

"I would like to talk to you. Remember when you said we could talk? Every time I see you, you are busy."

"Sorry, you're wrong." I had little patience for tout games this evening.

"You don't remember me . . . ?" I cut him off, knowing the rest of the sentence, which would be "from the hotel," at which point I was meant to assume he worked at my hotel. After gaining my confidence he would try to sell me something or borrow a small amount of money.

"That is impossible," I said firmly. "I have just arrived."

He faltered and fell back on an old standard.

"Where are you from?"

"New York City," I said. "Downtown Manhattan. I am not in a very good mood today."

He stopped, leaving me to finish my walk alone.

My sleep was fitful and I woke up early.

I took the destruction of the World Trade Center personally.

Most New Yorkers probably did. Time and subsequent events have numbed us to the memory of waking up to raw fear and uncertainty on September 12. How would America react?

But at least I was in a beautiful hotel room, instead of in my locked-down, asbestos-tainted home city. My small suite consisted of three rooms, although I really used only the bed and the bath.

Maybe I can salvage something from this trip to Zanzibar, I thought. I'd try again to book an excursion. I could go look at monkeys in nearby Jozani Forest.

Again I walked out into Stone Town. Again, I made the mistake of stopping by a television first to catch up on the news.

Suddenly, I no longer cared that I was in Zanzibar. I spent the entire day watching CNN and reading updates on the Internet.

A limited amount of automatic pilot kicked in, and I did manage to tour several small hotels. Emerson and Green was fantastic, but I was being horribly irresponsible by spending my limited funds on it. The Emerson and Green cook had a cheaper guesthouse that looked lovely in her brochure, but by my standards, it was still prohibitively expensive. The cheap hotels were mostly shabby and disgusting. I wasn't sure what I would do when I left Emerson and Green. Maybe I should give up on Zanzibar and head back to the mainland.

I had the unexpected problem of being prone to sudden bouts of weepiness. People were beginning to stare. Part of me wanted to accuse them of being callous—how dare they smile when so many people had died? But much as Americans barely understood what had happened in the 1994 Rwandan genocide or in the Angolan civil war I'd barely been aware of just two months ago, office buildings in New York were far away from the lives of people on the island of Zanzibar. It was a sad story but hardly a reason for them not to go about their business.

In the evening, I met Mubiana and Vicki for a drink on Emerson and Green's famous rooftop terrace. They'd sought me out earlier with, "We thought you could use some company." We reclined onto embroidered pillows, sipped drinks, and took in the sunset from the top of one of Stone Town's tallest buildings.

The view from the terrace—which overlooks mosques, corrugated metal roofs, church spires, alleyways, flat decaying whitewashed homes, and the Indian Ocean beyond—is renowned, but the real charm was in the audio.

The call to prayer sounded concurrently from several nearby mosques, semidroning but semimelodic, while bells jangled from a nearby Hindu temple. Zanzibar's population through the centuries had come from the Arabian Peninsula, Persia, Africa, India, and Europe. Traders had stopped here, many making Stone Town their home. Adventurers had launched expeditions into East and Central Africa from Zanzibar. The roots of the Swahili language are here, having evolved from the mixing of Arabic and the local Bantu language and culture. Zanzibar—sitting at the nautical crossroads of Asia, Africa, and the Arabian Peninsula—has been multicultural for four centuries.

My friends left Zanzibar the next day, and I finally left Emerson and Green to spend five times less on a budget room with shared toilets. It was a bring-your-own-sleeping-bag place, but I'd left my sleeping bag in storage in Dar Es Salaam. I spent a few night shivering under my towel, waking early to worry about the future of the world.

An old college friend emailed to remind me of a professor we'd had. The professor used to put his TV in the corner when the news was bad, and now I understood what he'd meant when he'd done this. The news had become repetitive and desperate, and it was less and less relevant, showing endless speculation by supposed experts, the same images of burning towers over and over, and second-guessing itself on the job it had done the day before. But I couldn't tear myself away. I'd alternate staring at CNN in a hotel lobby with dazed wanderings of the alleys of Zanzibar. I'd get lost, but it wouldn't matter. I'd keep walking, turning corners until I'd reach the sea.

The emails I got from home were startling. It was as if all my friends had suddenly woken up that morning and decided to try to write thriller novels. But of course the events they were reporting were not novice attempts at fiction. They were all reporting their personal experiences. Offices were closed, work had been brought to a standstill, the Captain America artist had temporarily stopped drawing in despair, and planes were grounded.

Debris littered downtown Manhattan. The revolving door I'd once anonymously shared with the singer of Deee-Lite at a music convention was gone, along with three thousand people and Lower Manhattan's most reliably clean public restroom.

Late one afternoon, I sat by the clear, aqua ocean, under a ceiling fan in an open-air restaurant. There was no enjoying Zanzibar, and I was just wasting money. I was miserable. Changing locations wouldn't help that. But at least if I were going to mope, I could do it somewhere cheaper. I'd go back to Dar Es Salaam tomorrow. Find a cheap hotel. Enjoy familiar comfort foods. I'd be closer to the airport in case planes started flying again and I had to rush home, and maybe, just maybe, there would be fewer men saying, *"Jambo,* blondie, what are you doing tonight?"

Chapter 7

Dazed in Dar

"I am very happy with you," declared Geoffrey, my regular waiter at Dar Es Salaam's Chef's Pride restaurant.

Perplexed, I stared at him from my seat on the open-air veranda. Had I over-tipped last night? He simply grinned back at me in response. Finally, I had to ask.

"Why are you happy with me?"

"Because you come here alone. And you are attractive. And you seem happy."

With that, he left to fetch me passion-fruit juice. Which was just as well, because otherwise I would have had to tell him the sad truth: I was not happy at all.

What was there to be happy about? I felt as if I'd woken up on the Planet of the Apes, staring at remnants of a collapsed New York icon while madness controlled the world.

Should I continue my trip, by heading north through Sudan to Egypt? What would happen next? Bombings? Sympathy? Rage? Would the world unite and move toward understanding, or was there more violence to come?

What was there more of in the world? Chimpanzees or damned dirty apes?

But the answers would not come quickly. While I moped around the sun-drenched, aging, concrete city of Dar Es Salaam, wondering if I should head north or just stop, the world numbly held its collective breath.

Taxi drivers and touts, attracted by my obvious "foreignness," still cheerfully tried to snare me with cries of *"Jambo,* where you from?" I wanted to smack them, throw a tantrum, or maybe sit down and bawl. *How could they be trying to sell me a trip to Zanzibar? Didn't they know we were in the middle of a massive world crisis?*

"Jambo," said a man, keeping pace with me as I left my hotel, passing under a sign that said: WOMEN OF IMMORAL TURPITUDE ARE STRICTLY NOT ALLOWED IN THE ROOMS.

"Jambo," I muttered.

"What do you do today? Go to Zanzibar?"

"No."

"Tomorrow?"

"Already been."

"Safari then?"

"No. Goodbye."

"Goodbye" didn't always work, but it often gave the touts pause. I'd take advantage of the moment to walk away briskly.

"*Jambo*," said a handicraft seller. "You look nice. Can I talk to you?"

I managed to disavow him of this notion by being thoroughly rude and ignoring him. I sought out the familiar—eating sandwiches in the air-conditioned, yellow interior of Subway or drinking coffee in the luxury hotel across from Citibank. I wanted comfort and I wanted to go home, but I couldn't now even if I had seriously tried. Air traffic was chaotic, and flights were booked for days.

"Welcome to Tan-*zan*-ia," people would say to me as I paced the streets between Subway and my hotel. And as I defrosted, I realized that not everyone was trying to sell me a trip to Zanzibar. Sometimes, they meant it. Even the day when the whole downtown ran on generator power and the municipal water supply cut off, the the friendliness of those around me was not dampened. It dawned on me slowly that if anyone were planning on bombing anyone else in the greater world, it was going to happen with or without my stressing about it. The best course of action, I decided, would be to preoccupy myself. I'd go to Serengeti and look at animals.

Could I really just casually go on safari? What other choice was there? Mope about in a crummy hotel or mope about with lions? I'd still be miserable on safari, but at least it would be someone else's responsibility to feed me.

Safaris to Serengeti begin from Arusha. I packed a peanut butter and jam sandwich for the bus ride. I'd head to Arusha in the morning.

The taxi driver who drove me to the bus station explained the finer points of emigration to me.

"No one in Tanzania wants to go to France. Or to Holland. No, it is three places: Germany, England, and America."

"Why?" I asked.

"Because these are countries where there is money to be made. And America is the best."

"Why is America better than the other countries?"

"Because," he said with a laugh. "In America, there are many Africans and everyone is an immigrant. No one will be mean to us. And it is easy to disappear. I could go to America and work very hard as a houseboy or taxi driver and no one would question me. No one would check my papers. Then I would come home a rich man."

I didn't have the heart to tell him about the cost of living in the United States, or about health insurance or hospital bills.

He dropped me at the bus terminal. I put on my backpack, reached down to pick up my water, and my backpack's forty pounds knocked me flat on my butt. To the taxi driver's credit, he did not laugh. But I did, feeling quite foolish but unable to play it as if I'd meant to fall on my bottom.

Along with a few Africans and five tourists, I boarded a "luxury" bus filled with mosquitoes and started the nine-hour trip to Arusha. The bus started up. The air-conditioning came on. A cockroach fell on me from the overhead vent, and we were off. For once I was traveling with a reputable bus company. No flat tires, no mechanical difficulties, and a timely arrival, though I slept through the trip and wouldn't have noticed if we had stopped by the side of the road.

Plenty of cockroaches infested East Africa, and I'd seen a fair number of them in hotels. I encountered several later that night, though I moved the next day to a nicer hotel in the residential outskirts of town.

Arusha had a reputation for especially persistent touts. I was pleased and surprised when I left the hotel and walked down a busy, tree-lined road to the town center. No Arushans greeted me with *"Jambo,* would you like to buy . . . ?" as they went about their daily lives. Children walked to school in their uniforms. Teenage boys in red-and-black checked Maasai blankets walked by in high-tech running shoes. A soccer game was in progress nearby.

"Karibu," said everyone who passed me. It meant "welcome" in Swahili, and in Arusha everyone said it nonstop. One African teenager who said *karibu* was dressed in baggy jeans, running shoes, and a floppy hat. He was the spitting image of an African American teenager—influenced by styles that in turn had been influenced by African culture of more than a hundred years ago.

I was feeling better about the state of the world after my time in Arusha, but nevertheless I had trouble working up the interest in going to look at animals. *What if people started bombing each other while I was gone?* But then I reminded myself that on the safari I was booked onto, someone else would feed me. Since it was "comfort camping," someone else would even put up my tent. I put my sleeping mat, mosquito net, Wet Ones, and peanut butter into storage at my hotel. The operator supplied the camp bed, and I hoped that peanut butter would not be required for "comfort camping."

I joined six tourists from England, Norway, and the United States in two 4x4s, one a Land Cruiser and the other a Land Rover. The drivers were two soft-spoken Tanzanian safari guides named Erasto and Wilfred. Our bags went on ahead on a separate truck, along with several porters and a cook.

After a few brief stops, we headed into Lake Manyara National Park, home of tree-climbing lions—or, as Wilfred said, "grass-sleeping lions if we're lucky," since lion-spotting is tough enough on the ground and far rarer in the trees.

Luck was not with us. We passed another Land Rover on the way into the park. Wilfred stopped our 4x4 to have a chat with the driver. This happens frequently on safaris, as drivers like to share information on sightings.

Although we tourists did not speak Swahili, it was obvious from the drivers' hand motions and from the slow shaking of the other driver's head that they were discussing the lack of wildlife in the park today.

"Did you see anything?" I imagined Wilfred was asking.

"Not a damn thing," the other driver probably responded. "You're a fool to even try."

We drove on anyway. Five of the seven of us passengers were fresh off the plane, and they got excited at baboons and the occasional giraffe. Their mood was infectious, and I found myself enthusiastic over the tiniest sliver of elephant butt. Even Wilfred looked slightly amused.

Finally, after spending a couple of hours spotting a few zebras, lots of baboons, and a few elephants, we reached the shores of Lake Manyara, where we were allowed to get out of the vehicles to walk around. Several other safari vehicles were also parked and dozens of tourists wandered around the coast.

As we scampered about, we noticed a Land Rover just up the road. An elephant approached. The Land Rover stopped and camera flashes went off. Then the elephant stopped right in front of the car, studied it, and circled it slowly. The passengers all ducked inside, as their heads had been poking out of the open top. The elephant blocked the road and stared hard at the Land Rover. The occupants must have been terrified. The enormous African elephant was larger than the car. Every tourist along the shoreline stared. What would happen?

Then, satisfied with scaring the daylights out of some tourists, the elephant lumbered on.

We left Lake Manyara, having seen no lions—tree-climbing or otherwise—and moved on to our campsite at Karatu. The paved road ended and we drove down the bumpy, dusty, potholed roads, lined with young Maasai boys in painted faces, hoping to make a tip by posing for a photo.

The line between commerce and tradition is unclear in many tribal areas. Traditionally, Maasai youths would paint their faces and dress up in black as a rite of passage. They would go out into the wilds to hunt an animal, perhaps a lion in the past, though this is now illegal. Nowadays, the youths would dress up in the same black outfits and hope that someone would stop to take a photo and then tip them. It made me uncomfortable, as I couldn't decide if this were a perfectly valid exchange of assets or some kind of cultural self-exploitation.

Everyone else appeared as uncertain about the situation as I did. No one asked Wilfred to pull over.

"Comfort camping" had sounded kind of silly to me, but I was amazed when we pulled into camp. The camp staff of five had raced ahead and set up enormous tents, canvas camp beds, and a dining table and chairs. They'd even cooked a dinner of beef stew over rice, and Chef William had written up a menu card. The campsite was nicer than most budget hotels I'd stayed in that year.

In the morning, leaving the staff to dismantle our tents and put our bags in the truck, we drove west toward Ngorongoro Crater. Children dressed in red tribal Maasai blankets waved as we passed by. Invariably, their waves turned to ghost-scribbling motions. These children were used to tourists throwing pens to them.

Our next stop was a Maasai village. The Maasai are the famous nomadic cattle-herding tribe of Kenya and Tanzania, well-known for their adherence to traditional lifestyles against the backdrop of modern Africa. They still dance and guard against lions, but now some of them do it for tourism.

"Take as many photos as you like," said Erasto. "They're free."

Or sort of free. We had again entered the strange world where tradition meets commerce.

In 1991, I had traveled down the Amazon on a converted steamer. We'd stopped at a tribal village, where the tribe obligingly changed out of shorts and T-shirts, put on grass skirts and beads, and did a dance. Members of the audience were (as usual) pulled up to participate, and then they bought trinkets before the tribe members changed back into their T-shirts.

In 2000, I went into Laos with a small group tour that took me into tribal Laotian villages. No one performed, but they welcomed us and let us take photos. In exchange, our leader brought them sacks of salt and flour. No one tried to sell us anything.

The Laos approach guaranteed a more "authentic" experience, but it was a slippery slope. How long before the village equated visitors with sacks of flour, and then realized they could get money instead? My comic book and pop culture/*Star Trek* roots were showing as I mused that Starfleet's prime directive of no interference in developing cultures was impossible to maintain.

You can't show tourists a culture without expecting their visit to influence the culture.

Our Maasai village in Tanzania was, at least, the real thing. It was a collection of small, circular mud huts—more than a dozen— encircled by a round, reed fence.

We'd seen plenty of Maasai nearby, all dressed in traditional bright red-and-black–checked blankets, so we knew the Maasai still dressed the part and were not changing clothes for our benefit.

One villager invited us in. He wore giant metal earrings, which dangled from quarter-size holes in his lobes. He followed us into the enclosure—a *Road Warrior*-esque Maasai world in the middle of the plain—and the girls of the village chanted while the boys jumped their Maasai dance. All were technically men and women, but they seemed very young to my Western eyes, in spite of already having spouses and children.

"The Maasai," explained our host, "can have several wives for one man. But each wife gets her own house."

The host invited us separately inside his tiny one-room hut of mud and reeds. It was shady and cool inside with just a small hole for a window, and it was way too small for a family of four—which is who lived there. His four-year-old daughter, her head shaved close, sat on a wooden stool and rested her chin on a dusty soccer ball.

Afterward, the Maasai tried to sell us trinkets, while the children asked for pens and coins. And several Maasai inquired about America.

"What will America do?" they asked excitedly. "Four airplanes, right?"

I felt a little guilty not buying anything, but two other tourists bought sticks that could purportedly be used to fend off lions, while a third traded an old watch for a blanket. The Maasai are huge fans of jewelry, and many keep several watches as adornments.

The Maasai had to be commended for their entrepreneurial spirit, but I wasn't too sure how I felt about attending their performance art or bringing them watches. I took refuge in the Land Cruiser and waited for the others, wrestling with the questions I knew were unanswerable. The others tourists seemed happy to participate. Maybe I was being overly sensitive.

We left the village/theater behind us and moved on to a small visitors center at Olduvai Gorge.

Renowned scientists Mary and Louis Leakey had made several groundbreaking discoveries of ancient human fossils at Olduvai Gorge. I vaguely remembered learning about it in elementary school. We looked at some exhibits and a few photos on the wall.

As usual, the Clinton family had beaten me there. Photos of Hillary and Chelsea adorned the walls from when they'd visited

Tanzania. This was an ongoing theme in my trip around the world, as I'd seen photos of one of the Clintons from their restaurant, museum, or shopping exhibitions across every continent.

A group of Tanzanian schoolkids were at Olduvai Gorge on a field trip. One of them ran by me and the Hillary Clinton photo, and I noted with the smug satisfaction of a comic-book editor that she wore a "Batman" baseball cap with her school uniform.

She boarded the school bus, and I focused on the graffitti scrawled into the dust on the back of the bus.

"Look, he's become some kind of Robin Hood," I said, pointing to the graffitti.

The rear window read OSAMA OSAMA, and the bumper said, I (HEART) OSAMA BIN LADEN.

We tourists watched silently as the bus pulled away. Too late, we remembered our cameras.

Chapter 8

Camping Tanzanian Style

"Rrrrrrroooooaaar," said a lion near our camp-site in the middle of the night. Actually, it didn't roar. Lions communicating with each other at night sound more like the adults on a Charlie Brown cartoon mixed with an irritated wookie.

I lay wide awake most of the night. I told myself that I'd survived enough nights in tents now and that lions were not clever enough to work out that there was a sleeping snack inside the nearest canvas wrapper. And I knew that they were not three feet away, which is how they sounded. Lion vocals carry. But all-night growling is not a soothing sound track conducive to deep sleep.

The lions were probably near the campground's tank of water.

Lions like water, and tourists like water. I found myself praising the Namibian campgrounds back in Etosha for their tall fences. Wilfred and Erasto had dozens of stories of chance encounters with bemused lionesses, all of which had been too bored or unhungry to bother eating them. We had been terrified by their stories over last night's dinner, and in the end, we'd all been a little disappointed when none of us had to shake a newly acquired Maasai stick at a curious lion.

Certainly, if it decided to, a lion could eat a human in minutes, and it does happen, particularly in areas with droughts or conflicts between wildlife and encroaching civilization. Farmers who sleep in their fields during harvest seasons run the risk of lion encounters. But tourists are usually in cars or tents, and when they come across a lion, it's frequently lazing around with a fat belly, having just snacked on a gazelle.

We took off on a crack-of-dawn game drive, and I was grumpy from lack of coffee. Yesterday had been such a wildlife-sighting dud, and we'd seen almost nothing, and certainly not any of the tree-climbing lions we'd been searching for in Lake Manyara.

"Maybe we'll see some lions today," said someone. We were in the Serengeti, after all, famous for its wild cats.

It didn't take long.

"That lion is in a tree!" exclaimed the usually calm Wilfred. He pulled over and stopped the 4x4.

An older male lion clung perched to a tree branch, more than ten feet above the ground. He shifted his weight uncomfortably. Below him was a herd of what looked like a hundred buffalo milling about.

"They've got him trapped," said Wilfred. "The buffalo are taking their revenge. A lion is no match for that many buffalo."

"Look, there's more!" said someone from the back seat.

Two lionesses stood across the road, hidden in the tall grass. They were clearly outnumbered by the buffalo and seemed uncertain of what they should do.

"Which one do you identify with, the lion or the buffalo?" asked one of the safari clients, a psychologist from Los Angeles.

I thought about it.

"The buffalo," I said. "I can't help but root for the underdog, and I'm not the king of the jungle."

"Now you understand that Osama bin Laden graffiti at Olduvai Gorge."

Indeed I did, and it was very troubling.

We left the tree-climbing lion to his fate and returned to camp. After a lunch of cold chicken, we started out again. That's when I learned a valuable lesson in animal-spotting. Some people are certainly better at animal-spotting than others. But in safari Africa, even the most nearsighted people—even those who have lost their glasses—can be ace spotters. All you have to do is look for the other cars.

Wilfred spotted an at-rest Land Rover, full of cameras and attached tourists.

"Leopard," exclaimed a sightseer. A leopard had lazily plastered himself over a large branch and was nearly camouflaged by his handsome spots.

I settled back and relaxed. I'd topped off my Big Five, not to mention seen hundreds of non–Big Five, and I was tired. Maybe I'd just zone out for the rest of the game drive.

But the Serengeti still had a few surprises. We came across a crowd of vultures on a tree branch (another popular spotting technique is to first spot vultures—the game will follow). Beneath them were four bloated lions, obviously overstuffed on dinner. A lioness was enthusiastically tearing into a hollowed-out half-buffalo nearby. She'd disappear into the buffalo's chest for minutes before reappearing for a quick breath. The vultures patiently waited their turn.

The lions came near our campsite again that night, but I was too tired to work up any fear. From within my tent, I heard a few gurgling whines before I fell into a deep sleep.

I'd been on a lot of safaris this year and was getting a little jaded. When I'd come to the Serengeti, I'd had low expectations. I'd seen so many giraffes, zebras, elephants, warthogs, and rhinos in Namibia and Zimbabwe. But the Serengeti was without equal when it came to cats. As we left camp, we spotted a gaggle of Land Rovers, their occupants happily clicking their cameras at two white-bellied cheetahs, who showed a total lack of interest in the proceedings around them. A stop at the Serengeti visitors center broke up the morning drive.

The afternoon game drive took us past our second leopard and third cheetah. We were still spotting lions, gazelles, warthogs, giraffes, and zebras too. They were so plentiful that they didn't even register. Every safari I've been on has one thing in common. You stop the car and take fifty photos of the first gazelle. An hour later, you cruise past the gazelle at the top speed allowed in the park because you are far more interested in the next toilet than in the next three hundred gazelles.

Wilfred provided that afternoon's most unexpected entertainment. He inexplicably surprised all of us with a lecture on the politics of Sweden. Encouraged by our interest, he then proceeded to tell us about the economics of getting a used car into Tanzania. He'd never done it himself, but he knew people who'd bought cars in Dubai or Jeddah and then shipped them back. He'd heard rumors of some who had even managed to smuggle their cars in.

Finally, Wilfred, like Shawn back in Namibia, had his own ideas about the animal kingdom. "Big Five," he said with a sigh. "Everyone wants to see Big Five. But I want to see a mongoose."

"Er, why?" This made no sense to me.

"It's like this," he explained. "Mongoose eats snake. Snake scares lion. The mongoose is the true king of the jungle."

Years later, when I was living in the Ugandan bush, I'd hear a similar tale from my friend Celsius.

"Have you ever heard the story of why the puss-cat is always with the woman?"

I hadn't, and Celsius—the Uganda Wildlife Authority electrician at Murchison Falls National Park—told it to me over a Coke one evening (once I'd established that a puss-cat is a common housecat).

"Once upon a time," Celsius began, "the puss-cat lived in the forest. The puss-cat is a small cat and it was not able to feed itself because the other animals took away all the food. So the puss-cat became friends with the lion. It thought that the lion was the strongest animal in the forest, so there would always be food. And the lion let the puss-cat eat the extra food when he was done.

"Then one day, along came a buffalo. And he chased away the lion and took his food. So the puss-cat became friends with the strong buffalo instead, and the buffalo let him eat his food. Now the puss-cat thought he was friends with the strongest animal.

"Then one day, a man came into the forest. And he killed the buffalo for its meat. And the puss-cat said, 'Ehh, the man is stronger than the lion or the buffalo,' and it attached itself to the man and became friends with the man.

"Then the puss-cat knew that he really was with the strongest creature and he would always be fed. But then the man arrived home. And he laid down his spears and goods at the foot of his wife, and she allowed the man to enter the house. So then the puss-cat knew that the woman was stronger than the lion and the man, and to this day the puss-cat attaches itself to the woman."

Several blanket-clad Maasai women (catless) were walking alongside the road as we left the Serengeti. Wilfred slowed down and wound down his window.

"Where have you been?" He asked the women in Swahili.

"Shopping at Kimba Village." The women were coming back from the Maasai equivalent of a day at the mall.

A few hours later, Wilfred pulled into a crowded, dirty campground on the edge of Ngorongoro Crater. There'd be no roaring lions here, just a lot of laughing into the night as our neighbors consumed beer and swapped safari tales.

"Marie, how long have you been driving?" he asked.

"Seventeen years or so," I replied.

"I can tell. You've been driving all day."

Subconsciously, probably because I'd been riding in the passenger seat in a right-hand–drive car, I'd been pressing an imaginary brake as we drove across the grassy plains. I hadn't even noticed, and I was still not totally convinced. I was pretty sure I'd heard him make the same joke earlier to the Norwegian client.

In the morning, we headed down into the crater.

Ngorongoro Crater is a unique ecosystem—and one of Tanzania's most visited parks—that is famous for its animals, which are spoiled rotten by year-round access to grass and water. The wildebeests from the Serengeti migrate to Kenya during the dry season—the Ngorongoro wildebeests lazily stay home.

We'd been astonishingly lucky so far, with our tree lion, two leopards, feasting lions, and three cheetahs. We jokingly demanded a rhino sighting from Erasto, who with great seriousness reminded us that the wild was not a zoo.

We drove down into the crater.

It was a disheartening morning. We saw a few zebras, some wildebeests, and the occasional warthog. The cold turned to hot sun, and flies set upon us. We were all hungry and dehydrated. We were carrying plenty of water, but we weren't drinking enough. No one wanted to make a toilet run in the middle of lion country. You couldn't just run out of the car and duck behind a bush. It involved a lot of "holding it."

Despite Erasto's admonition, we'd all been hoping to spot a rhino but were disappointed to see almost nothing.

Finally, after four hours of fruitless looking, we decided that brunch might be an appealing prospect, and we turned toward a picnic area.

En route were two consolation prizes. The first was a hippo pool. I'd seen hundreds of hippos at this point, and I thought there were no hippo surprises left. I was wrong, as the Ngorongoro hippos were all enjoying their morning by doing Eskimo rolls in the water. Their feet and pink bellies would poke out of the water, alternating with broad gray backs as they whirled around, splashing loudly. They were clearly having fun swimming in the hot Tanzanian afternoon.

After hippo-watching until we were too jealous of their fun to stare anymore, we moved on to an algae-colored lake that was infested with bright pink flamingoes, so our disappointment had lessened by the time we got to the picnic area. The toilets there actually flushed, demonstrating what the wildebeests already knew—that Ngorongoro had plenty of water.

Do Not Feed the Animals, read the sign by the lakeside picnic spot. I barely noticed it. There were lots of warnings like this in Africa's national parks.

"Be careful of the black kites," warned Erasto. "They will try to take your food."

This registered only slightly with me—I should keep an eye on my food. *Yeah, right, whatever.*

Our brunch consisted of cold vegetable empanadas, spicy fried meatballs, and greasy "sweet pancakes." Lunch every day featured sweet pancakes, a greasy fried dough that I was not at all fond of. I quietly placed mine on a nearby rock. The birds were welcome to it.

A minute later, an enormous kite swooped in. It snatched the empanada from my hand and took it to a distant branch before I comprehended what it had done. Another one went for Lucy's food, but she hid her empanada under her shirt.

Erasto chided me for feeding the birds with an "I told you so" remark. I was too surprised—not to mention guilty as charged—to marshal a reply.

I took a second empanada, guarded it carefully, and managed to down half of it before a kite swooped in low over my shoulder and snatched it from my hands, even though I held it close to my chest. Wilfred lost his sweet pancake in much the same way, although I suspected he had deliberately lost it so that I wasn't the only one feeling foolish.

The kites left us for a Barcelona lesbian travelers' club that arrived for its own picnic, and we fled the birds, energized for more game-spotting.

It didn't take long before someone spotted the usual "rock rhino," a rock formation mistaken initially for a rhino. Other infamous sightings included the warthog-rhino and the elephant-rhino. Finally, the psychologist spotted two dark-gray blotches in the distance, but this time they had horns on their noses.

"Rhino!" he declared triumphantly. They were, and while they were too distant for a good long examination, they genuinely were rhinos. Now everyone in the group had seen the Big Five.

I'd had enough now. I'd overdosed on game drives and was all animaled-out now. I wondered if perhaps a better way to economize my time might be to ditch the last few days of game drives and go to Arusha early to meet my friend Paul.

Paul was leading Kilimanjaro trips for a British firm and was in Arusha until early October. If I stuck to my schedule, I'd see him briefly on the evening of the 28th. I wanted to spend more time with him than that, having seen so few real friends all year, and I was thinking of staying an extra day in Arusha—but then I'd be cutting into my tight mountain gorilla–viewing/Masai Mara ballooning schedule. Something had to give.

The solution, I decided, was to leave this group to catch a morning bus to Arusha, spend a few days with Paul, and then head to Nairobi to connect through to a bus to Uganda.

"Stop," someone yelled, interrupting my silent planning. "Cheetah!"

We backed up. A bored cheetah sat up on a mound of dirt next to the road. He shot us a few glances and then turned his back to us.

After another circuit to look at more zebras and elephants, we stopped at a toilet block.

Vervet monkeys infested the parking lot, and they kept crawling through open roofs and into safari Rovers. Tourists would coo and crowd around the trucks to take photos, leaving the monkeys few escape routes. This agitated the monkeys, which ran around the cars wildly, managed to escape, and then approached other Rovers to begin the fun all over again.

We drove up a dusty, horrendous road out of the crater, past the campground on the rim. I'd head to Arusha in the morning.

Chapter 9

Busabout

Erasto the safari guide was fretting. What if a taxi driver ripped me off in Arusha?

"You can take the Ngorongoro Crater bus," he said, "but the taxi ride in Arusha . . ."

"I know how tourist prices work," I assured him. "Don't worry, I've gotten myself this far. I can catch a taxi."

Erasto drove me to the bus stop in the center of Karatu town, and then he walked me onto the bus and deposited me into a long padded seat next to a student. The other passengers on the dilapidated bus— a combination of Tanzanians dressed in clothes similar to mine and Maasai dressed in checkered blankets—did stare, but it was surely because I was being escorted and not because I was a stranger. We were not exactly off the tourist route.

For $3, I got a seat for the hundred-kilometer ride to Arusha. The dirt road—rumored to have been rebuilt since—was pitted, and red dust spewed into my nostrils, turning them orange. The potholes were not large enough to park the bus in, but a sedan could quite comfortably sit in many of them. The roads hadn't changed since my drive out here a week ago. They were the same uncomfortable roads I'd driven over with Wilfred in the Land Rover. The only differences were the shock absorbers, and that in the Land Rover, there hadn't been Maasai standing in the aisle. The Maasai perched next to me kept tossing his blanket back over his shoulder, and it kept hitting me in my face as I read my book, a book about the source of the Nile that I'd picked up in a shopping mall in Dar. The student giggled. I tried to maintain a dignified look of not being bothered.

The ride took almost four hours before we stopped in Arusha. The Maasai slowly disembarked, the seated passengers followed, and my feet touched the paved bus lot. I hired a taxi (without much fussing, in spite of Erasto's worries) and headed to Arusha Naaz Hotel.

On my frantic search for a decent hotel the last time I'd been in Arusha, I'd found that Arusha Naaz was the nicest cheapie. At $20 a night, it was far more expensive than the $8–12 set, but it was centrally located.

I checked in, washed the orange dust from my hands and face, and hurried to the Internet café to check for messages from Paul.

He'd sent me an email while I'd been out looking at lions. I replied, told him where I was, and he strolled in the Internet café doors ten minutes later.

We hugged, laughing. I hadn't seen Paul in more than a year—or even a familiar face in three months—and it was great to have someone around who knew me well and didn't have to ask the standard traveler's questions: Where are you from? How long have you been traveling? Where will you go next? I often joked that I'd have small trading cards printed with answers to Frequently Asked Questions on the back of them. Paul and I went first to a coffee shop, then to Arusha's Ethiopian restaurant, and lazily bantered about our plans and about the future of the world.

A photo of Bill Clinton hung on the wall of the Ethiopian restaurant. The Clintons were always a step ahead of me.

Paul had been my friend Nikki's codriver on my '98 Dragoman overland trip from Kathmandu to Damascus. Before that he'd driven for an overland company in Africa. We'd both been new to India and the Middle East in '98, and we had bonded enough to keep in touch when our schedules allowed—which had so far been three times, once in Oxford, once on the Isle of Wight, and once in California. Paul had found a niche for himself that enabled him to aid society and satisfy his own wanderlust. He alternated taking teens on extended leadership-development trips through South America with leading charity fundraising trips. I was, however, utterly clueless about how to proceed with my life once my round-the-world project ended. I was jealous. Paul had direction. My own direction would expire at midnight on December 31.

As I walked through the lobby of Arusha Naaz hotel after

leaving Paul, I noticed two hotel employees staring with fascination at the computer. Glancing over their shoulders, I saw that they were intently playing and replaying an animated map of the flight paths of the planes that had hit the World Trade Center. They looked at me, caught my glance, and giggled. I hastily walked by, disturbed. *What was so fascinating?*

I ran errands the next day, stocking up on film and mailing postcards, and met Paul in the evening.

This time we ate at an Italian restaurant on the edge of town, where an African band played "La Bamba"—singing it in Spanish, not Swahili.

"How hard is it to climb Kilimanjaro?" I asked Paul. It's Africa's tallest mountain, but fit nonclimbers can make it to the top unless they are overcome by altitude sickness. People often assume they can make it, but the problem with altitude sickness is that you don't know how altitude will affect you until you're up in the thick (or thin) of it. I'd had vague plans to attempt the climb before September 11, after which I had wanted only to sulk and not to attempt anything especially ambitious.

"Every time I do it, I think it's the hardest thing I've ever done," said Paul with a laugh. I was glad I hadn't tried the climb. If athletic Paul had trouble making it to the summit, I wouldn't have had a prayer.

I'd booked the shuttle bus to Nairobi for the next morning, but my plan didn't exactly work out. I stood in front of the hotel, chatting with a newspaper vendor. Fifteen minutes after watching the shuttle sail by—I'd assumed it would return after making the rounds to other hotels, but it had not—the newspaper vendor became worried.

"The shuttle is never this late," he said matter-of-factly. "You need to call them."

I returned to the receptionist. She called the shuttle company. It did not have a record of my booking.

"Oh, well," I said. "Where do the minibus taxis leave from?"

She stared at me with an expression of horror.

"No, no, you cannot take a *dala-dala* minibus. Tourists should take the shuttle. It is much nicer."

Fortunately, the hotel manager was listening.

"The Peugeot taxis are not bad. You can take a Peugeot."

He whisked me into the hotel's car and instructed the driver to take me to the shared Peugeot taxis.

"You are our guest. There is no charge for the lift."

Ten minutes later, I was on the way to the Kenyan border. I sat in the front passenger seat of an eight-passenger Peugeot, next to a nine-year-old uniformed Indian boy who was on his way to boarding school. His grandmother had reached over me at the bus stop, cooing over her grandson, who looked patient but exasperated with her attention. She'd handed him a sandwich. As soon as she'd left, he'd negotiated with a vendor to buy a pair of headphones. He plugged them into his CD player, turned up the volume, and stared ahead.

Behind us were three Maasai, one businessman, and two large women, who were crammed into the rear seats. One of the Maasai was wearing a safari vest under his checkered red-and-black blanket. He kept up a running commentary throughout the short trip to the border, and apparently he was quite hilarious as all the other passengers were in stitches. Unfortunately, all of these excellent jokes were relayed in Swahili, and all I understood was "Tanzania" and "Nairobi."

The Peugeot stopped only once for two of the Maasai to pee by the side of the road, and it reached the border at the same time as the shuttle. The nine-year-old kid got out of the Peugeot and disappeared, along with the Maasai. I had my passport stamped out on the Tanzanian side before being driven (with my bag) to the Kenyan side.

The kid reappeared out of nowhere.

"How much is the exchange rate?" He addressed me urgently.

I shrugged. He looked at me with an expression of surprise and disgust. I was an adult; surely I was supposed to know these things. He rolled his eyes and walked away.

I shouldered my pack and stood in line behind the shuttle passengers before being stamped into Kenya. I walked across the Kenyan border and boarded a new Peugeot bound for Nairobi. The total cost for a shuttle trip was $20. The total for me doing the same trip by public transport? $7. And surely the shuttle did not come with Maasai comedians.

The only disadvantage was that the Peugeot arrived in the worst part of Nairobi instead of dropping me off at a hotel. This was one time when I had to overcome my natural cheapskate tendencies that steered me toward walking. I caught a taxi to the hotel I was planning to stay in next week and stored my bag. My plan now was to travel to Uganda on the overnight bus and return to Nairobi in a week. I saw no point in carrying my camping gear along.

From the hotel, I hired a taxi for the afternoon and went to the Akamba bus booking office.

The booking agent had some bad news for me. Tonight's buses were sold out.

"Are there other buses?" I asked.

"Sure, Busscar."

"What??"

"Busscar."

"Can you write that down, please?"

"Buscaar, River Road." In block letters, he laboriously misspelled the name.

Off I went to River Road.

"No," said the River Road Busscar agent. "That bus is booked from the other office, on Accra Road."

Off again, this time to decrepit Accra Road, which is more a wide dirt alley than a road. The surrounding buildings featured signs advertising many different bus lines. A tiny sign down a narrow lane said: BUSSCAR.

"That's it!" I said. My taxi driver stopped and let me out. I bought a ticket from an Arabic man in a snack shop.

"Where does the bus leave from?" I asked.

"Right here." The man motioned outside the door.

The only problem, I realized, was that I'd never find the place again in the dark. The bus was leaving at 8 PM.

"I will bring you," announced my taxi driver, who had patiently driven me all over town that afternoon. We agreed he'd be at the hotel at seven thirty, and then he dropped me off at Barclays Bank, where

I delightedly used the ATM to take funds directly out of my home checking account. I hadn't seen an ATM like that in a month, and I had been living off ATM Visa cash advances, which I'd pay off online.

At the arranged time, I left the hotel for the bus station. I looked uncertainly for my taxi driver.

"Here I am," said a man.

He looked different, but it was dark. But even stranger—his car was different.

"Earlier you had a station wagon," I said doubtfully.

"My brother's," he said. Uncertainly, I got in. We left and I listened carefully for some evidence that I was in the right car.

"Which airline is it again?" asked the driver casually.

Argh. I rolled my eyes with consternation at myself for making a novice's mistake. I'd known he was not the right driver, but I hadn't trusted my instincts.

"You are not my driver. Turn around now."

"What?"

"Back to the hotel. I am not going to the airport. You lied. You are not my driver."

He quietly drove me back.

My original driver was MIA, but plenty of taxis wait outside hotels in Nairobi, as they do in cities all over the world. Another driver managed to get me to the Busscar stop, and he wouldn't leave me until I was safely on the bus. Accra Road at night is not a safe place for anyone, especially a bag-carrying tourist.

The conductor who took my ticket issued me some fear-inspiring instructions.

"Remember my face," he said. "Give your bag to no one else. There are thieves here."

I boarded the bus. It could have been a lot worse. It was an older bus—by no means a nice coach like the Scandinavia Express coaches that would ply this route a few years later—but the seats reclined and I had scored a back double seat to myself. I was the only non-African on board and caused a bit of a stir at first. But the other passengers got bored with staring at me and soon went about the business of sleeping.

The sleeping didn't last long, though. The road deteriorated, and the bus lurched around all night. Every time I drifted off, the bus would jolt into a crater, sending my head smacking against the window or just sideways, snapping through the air.

We stopped early in the morning. It was still dark out. The bus engine cut off. We were at the border, but the border wasn't open yet. Finally, a chance to sleep. Briefly. The border opened forty minutes later. After getting stamped out of Kenya, I followed the lead of three Ugandans and brushed my teeth in a ditch. We all changed money with guys in homemade uniforms—long green cotton shirts with cutoff sleeves and the words "money changers" stenciled on the back.

We boarded the bus and drove west into Uganda as the sun rose. The road became smooth and paved, and I opened my eyes to get a first look at Uganda.

Green, I thought. The countryside was rich and beautiful, its color deepened by an unexpectedly early rainy season.

Occasionally the bus would stop at a police checkpoint, only to be mobbed by snack sellers, who'd push fried-meat-on-sticks through the open windows. Newspapers were also popular, although they were for reading, not eating. The snack sellers, like the money changers, all wore similar uniforms.

Ugandans, I thought, *dig uniforms.*

Sometimes traveling salesmen came on board to extol the virtues of a certain product—little packets of soap or vitamins or whatever they'd managed to acquire in bulk. The Kenyan man in front of me bought one of everything offered.

Bundles of charcoal or huge bunches of green bananas—which are ground into a starchy food called *matoke*—were pushed along the road on the backs of bicycles.

At one stop, a young man was selling water. He stuck a bottle at me through the window. I waved him away. Bored, he struck up a conversation.

"Are you born again?"

"No." I was startled by the question.

"But aren't you American?"

"Yes, but not all Americans are born again."

"All of the Americans in Uganda are."

The bus pulled away. The conversation was ended.

Chapter 10

Hakuna Matatu

The Busscar conductor grinned devilishly as he pranced around the Kampala bus terminal while wearing my backpack. I'd been delayed behind thirty-seven other passengers who had taken their time leaving the bus—there's "no hurry in Africa"—and he'd gotten bored while holding my bag. I laughed, relieved him of his burden, and walked alone out of the bus-park gate.

What a sight awaited me! The Busscar garage overlooked Kampala's "Old Taxi Park."

In the countries of East Africa, as in many countries all over the world, public transport is generally found in shared minibus taxis—*matatus* in Swahili—that run "when full." "Full" means fourteen passengers, one driver, one conductor, and countless babies and toddlers. In Uganda, passengers are legally required to wear seatbelts. In reality, this law is usually enforced only on long-distance routes and even then, often only the passengers in the front seat buckle up.

Kampala has two taxi parks. One—the newer taxi park—serves destinations to the south and west. The other—the one I now looked at—services the north and east. Neither of them looked especially new. They might be more aptly titled "Old" and "Older."

Hundreds of blue-and-white minivans lined the big, dirty city block in front of me, while conductors hollered out destinations. A thick smell of diesel permeated the air. Vendors carrying an assortment of items—socks, watches, bottled water, pens, flip-flops, keychains—plied their trades as they circled constantly through the maze of taxis, shoving products through any open window.

Dazed from both lack of sleep and the onslaught of diesel fumes, I turned right and aimed for "Tourist Hotel." At $25 a night, it wasn't cheap by my standards, but it featured standard-hotel quality in a central location. I was in Kampala for only a few days, just long enough to get the permit I needed to see the mountain gorillas in the southwest of the country.

After checking in, I headed to a small café for a banana muffin and coffee. The walls there were covered with newspaper articles about coffee exporting.

Coffee prices were at an all-time low. Farmers were putting the blame on Vietnam, which they said had flooded the market, and on three multinationals for making a fortune but passing none of the proceeds back to the farmers.

Why, at a time when a cup of coffee would often cost me $3 at home, was none of this profit making it back to the growers? Consumers paid a lot while growers got practically nothing. I was missing a large part of the puzzle.

"Jesus, Jesus, Jesus . . ." Christian radio played in the café, an incongruous sound track for my Ugandan coffee revelation. A man from the American West could be heard detailing the events leading up to his personal salvation.

"Hello. How are you?" A quiet voice intruded into my reading of one of Uganda's two daily newspapers.

I looked up to see if I were being addressed. A college-age Ugandan woman in blue jeans and a T-shirt sat down across from me. It is considered polite to speak quietly in Uganda, which means that not only was I, like most foreigners—*mzungus*—considered rude, but I was then doubly rude when I would loudly say, "What? Can you speak up?"

"Fine. How are you?" I responded cautiously.

She smiled and said, "I am Regina," as if I knew her.

"I am Marie." This often results in some interesting responses, as the name Marie is unknown in Uganda and is instead pronounced as Mary. Sometimes people respond with a sage nod and the words: "Mary, mother of god." One woman had broken out in a chorus of "Mary Had a Little Lamb." Regina didn't seem too worried about how to pronounce it.

"I would like to be your friend," stated Regina.

I pondered this for a moment, without responding.

"How long have you been in Uganda?"

"Not long. I'm a tourist."

"Oh. Where are you from?"

"United States. Do you live in Kampala?"

"Yes. I have been here my whole life. I have never been outside Uganda. I have not even finished secondary school because I do not have the money for school fees."

Ah. So she was looking for a sponsor. I felt put on the spot and uncomfortable. Here I was, about to spend $250 on a gorilla permit, while this girl was asking me to pay for her education.

"I have the same problem," I responded. "I would like to finish my schooling and get a master's, but I cannot afford even the cheapest school."

Our worlds were so different. I was talking about not being able to swing thousands of dollars while she was dealing in hundreds. But for both of us, the education was unreachable.

"I understand," said Regina.

We sat in silence for a minute. I was hoping she'd leave, that my remark about not being able to afford my own school would tell her that I wasn't going to pay for hers. I always wrestle with questions of aid on the road. I believe in spending money in local economies, but I also believe that direct handouts are not productive. The idea of the tourist as Santa Claus seems wrong to me, designed mostly to make the tourists feel good about themselves as they hand out candy, while the local kid gets rotten teeth out of the deal. *But education? Was that different?* I felt squeamish.

"I'm going to read my newspaper, okay?" Maybe she'd take the hint.

"Okay." Regina sat and stared at me until I offered her part of my *Daily Monitor.* She studied it, reading the newspaper carefully.

I finished the paper and the muffin.

"I'm leaving now." I stood up. Regina rushed through to the end of my paper and handed it back to me.

"I have a question," she said.

"Yes?"

"Come outside. I will ask you outside."

That was too much for my self-protection mechanisms and I didn't even think before the words were out of my mouth.

"Whatever it is, I am not interested," I said firmly.

Regina nodded and left.

I gave her a few minutes' head start and then trailed her for a bit. *Where was she going now? What had she wanted? Was she a con artist or was she a student willing to try anything to finance her education? Was I wrong to not help people? Was I a walking ATM? Should I be sharing my puny income with Regina? Should I be accepting personal responsibility for slavery, the price of coffee, and colonialism? Who should be accepting it? Was my plan to travel and spend money in local economies as my own small way of helping delusionary? And on a more global scale, were aid and development helping or hurting Africa?*

I wouldn't know the answers to these discomforting questions today. Perhaps I'd never know the answers. Scholars with far more awareness of the complexities of aid and development have never come up with satisfactory answers, so I didn't expect to state a simple one-size-fits-all solution today. My personal philosophy has always been the same: Each situation must be dealt with on a case-by-case basis. Aid and development are not universally good or universally bad. Blanket statements that I have heard about all aid and development interference needing to "get out of Africa" are naive.

Abandoning my ethics questions, I headed out to Kampala's outskirts to check out a backpacker's lodge. I was running low on funds and didn't think I should stay in the Tourist Hotel when I returned to Kampala.

I boarded a minibus taxi in the New Taxi Park. We drove about fifteen minutes west.

"Stop!" I said when I saw the lodge up ahead.

We went sailing by my stop.

A young Ugandan woman noticed my distress.

"Mah-sow!" she said. The driver pulled over immediately.

Like all children of the television generation, I know a few words of Swahili. *Uhuru* means "freedom." As in Uhura, the miniskirted communications officer on James T. Kirk's USS *Enterprise,* responsible for the first interracial television kiss. Later, Disney and Elton John taught us in *The Lion King* that *hakuna matata* means "No worries." And of course everyone knows the word *safari,* which actually means "journey," not "look at animals."

But Swahili is spoken in only part of Uganda, with Luganda, English, or tribal languages spoken in the rest. And *mah-sow* (spelled "maso awo" in Luganda) seems to mean "just ahead" no matter which language you actually spoke. Everyone (but me) knew the word *mah-sow,* and now I knew it too.

On the return trip, I inadvertently boarded the school bus.

The minibus was nearly empty when I flagged it down. A few

minutes later, we stopped in front of a small private primary school. A teacher gave some coins to the conductor and ushered six uniformed children onto the bus. The smallest child could not step up to board, so the conductor had to lift him onto the front seat.

The six children took up only two seats, as they sat squished together. We drove along for a few minutes, and then a medium-size kid squeaked. *"Mah-sow!"*

The driver pulled the taxi over and the conductor opened the sliding door. A mother was waiting in front of a three-walled butcher shop. Her two children hopped out of the minivan and she smiled at them as she took their hands.

We proceeded until the other kids said, *"Mah-sow."*

The rest of the children disembarked. The other few passengers helped to lift the kids to the sidewalk. Several walked together down a dirt road. The conductor took two kids by the hands and walked them across the street before returning to us. No one complained about the delay. It's all a part of a typical shared taxi journey in Uganda.

Chapter 11

Gorillas of the Bad Gas

Ugandans must have bladders of steel, I thought, shifting anxiously in my seat every time the decrepit old Silver Royal bus hit a pothole in the dirt road. I'd boarded the bus at 6 AM in the dusty bus park in downtown Kampala. It was now after four in the afternoon. Stops were only long enough to allow passengers time to embark or disembark, and sometimes the bus roared off while a passenger hung from the bars along the door, cheerfully scrambling to get both feet solidly through the bus entrance.

"You pray for a flat tire," Mark the overland driver would tell me later in Ethiopia, "just so you can pee."

He was right. Mark had been driving overland trucks through Africa for a decade, and he was seldom wrong, especially about Uganda, the country he loved most. In a few years, I'd covet his lifestyle, as he enjoyed a job, a house, and permanent residency in cool, laid-back Jinja, a lakeside town fifty miles east of Kampala.

But for now, I had carefully taken only tiny sips of water throughout the day. The Ugandan passengers had been less cautious. Between constant "welcomes" addressed to me, many of them had guzzled sodas that had been shoved through the open bus windows by eager sellers, who also hawked grilled meat on a stick. I knew we were still several hours from our destination, but I was not too anxious. By now I'd learned that flat tires occur with astounding regularity in East Africa. I'd get my toilet break soon enough.

Our flat tire du jour took place in the late afternoon. We were in a rural area in southern Uganda. There were few cities in the lush, green equatorial countryside and villages often consisted of only a strip of concrete roadside shops and a few mud huts. We'd lost our tire next to a tiny tea shop that had a doorless pit latrine out back. I visited it with relief, to the amusement of a dozen local children, who giggled as I made a beeline for the three-sided mud block. The other passengers lined up to use the toilet as well. Standard operating procedure appeared to be to wait behind its walls.

The children were as confused by my presence as I was by the Green Bay Packers sweatshirt and green skirt worn by one of them. Why was a foreigner standing by an old, broken bus alongside a dirt road in rural Uganda? I wanted to explain but did not know the words. The official language of Uganda is English, but Luganda and Swahili—

along with assorted tribal languages—dominate the countryside. I opened my guidebook and pointed to a photo of a mountain gorilla.

"*Ngagi!*" shrieked the children. They scattered playfully in mock fear and then returned, crowding around me for a better look at the photo. I'd been reading Dian Fossey's *Gorillas in the Mist*. *Ngagi*, she'd written, was the Swahili word for "gorilla."

I think I managed to convey to the children that I was taking an old bus from Kampala to Butogota to see twelve of the three hundred mountain *ngagi* in Bwindi Impenetrable National Park. The kids easily accepted that a foreigner had been plopped down into their midst. They lost interest in me, instead eagerly tearing through my guidebook to look at all the animal photos. They'd no doubt learned about zebras, elephants, and giraffes in school—Ugandan primary school is free for up to four children in a family—but these young children would probably not get to visit their country's national parks until they were adults. Some of them might never see an elephant in the wild, any more than an American kid would run across a buffalo or wolf.

The ground was soft beneath our feet. Rainy season had come early this year, turning the usually passable dirt road into a pit of mud. The projected ten-hour bus ride was turning into a painful thirteen-hour journey.

Still, I was pleased with the bus. Although it was old, slow, and uncomfortable, it was the cheapest way to get to Bwindi.

Initially, I had looked into organized tours out of both Nairobi and Kampala. But information had been difficult to find, and outfitters too expensive. My guidebook offered sketchy details

of rumored public transportation, but concrete evidence had
come from a Kampala hostel's website. Yes, there was a daily bus
from Kampala to the village of Butogota. From there, I'd have to
hire a pickup-truck taxi to drive me the last ten miles to Bwindi
Impenetrable National Park.

"Let's go!" The bus conductor interrupted my thoughts.

The tire had been changed. The engine roared to life, and the
smell of diesel blew through the village, mixing with the odor of
charcoal that always wafts through the air in rural Uganda, despite
environmentalists' campaigns to persuade people to switch to natural
gas. The girl in the secondhand Packers shirt shoved my guidebook
back into my hand, and I scrambled back to my seat against the
half-closed window. The man sitting next to me—who had initially
boarded carrying a bowl of hot soup and a transistor radio—gave
up his seat to a mother and baby who had been perched in the aisle
astride a stack of bicycle tires. He smiled, opened his knees wide, and
bounced on the bike tires. He tuned in some Ugandan Christian pop
on his staticky radio.

The bus is the lifeline in rural Africa, and any person with a
flapping hand is a potential bus stop. Buses usually race along at
breakneck speeds, barreling down on smaller vehicles and easily
intimidating drivers into moving aside. Then, a hand alongside the
road flaps. The bus screeches to a halt. The passenger boards with help
from the conductor. The bus races on.

There was no racing along the pitted road today. Progress
was slow. Rain began and then stopped. Evening fell and the sky
darkened. I'd long since finished every book in my daypack and had

quit being entertained by the huge bundles of cloth or groceries that other passengers had brought on board. I'd spoken to every rotund, middle-aged woman dressed in colorful clothing on board, mostly about their grandchildren or the distant relatives of theirs who had once been to New York. We were all tired and had run out of small talk after thirteen hours together.

Then the lights went out. All of them. The headlights quit illuminating the road ahead. The interior lights were out. Not even a speck of light showed on the dashboard. Streetlights are unheard of in rural Uganda. We were engulfed in total darkness.

I felt alarm rise within me, but faster than I could begin to worry, the driver sensibly applied the brakes without altering his course. We rolled to a stop. A flashlight came on in the front of the bus. The driver and the conductor got out. All passengers were silent, watching as the team opened the hood and worked on the electrical system by a wavering light.

Whatever they did worked. The lights came on, both inside and outside. The bus started. We reached town only ten minutes later.

Everyone disembarked at the end of the line in Butogota, not with excitement or any sense of victory, but simply with exhaustion.

Taxi drivers met the bus, and within an hour I was in a concrete dining room next to a shared *banda*—or hut—at Bwindi's Community Restcamp. A teenage Ugandan boy gave me a bucket of water to wash off the day's filth and then served me spaghetti by candlelight.

"Do the gorillas ever come to the camp?" I asked him.

"Sometimes they come to see us. They wander into the yard. I am sure that they know me."

"Will you please sign the register?" he asked, motioning to a guest book that sat in the hallway.

"Can I just write my name without my nationality or home address?" I realized that the government probably required the hostel to keep a record of my passport number, nationality, and vital details, but I also worried that this book sat out in the public hallway and that anyone could view it. The eight American, British, and New Zealander tourists kidnapped and killed in Bwindi in 1999 were among fourteen singled out for their English-speaking abilities, and they were bludgeoned or macheted during a daylong forced march. More than a hundred extremist rebel Hutus from Rwanda—still fighting from a base in nearby Democratic Republic of Congo—had crossed the border specifically to send a message of fear to America and Britain but also to damage Uganda, which had aided the Tutsis and moderate Hutus in bringing a halt to the 1994 Rwandan genocide. The rebel Hutu militia had succeeded in damaging Uganda's tourist income for a time. Tourism had dropped off. It had still not completely recovered when I arrived.

Uganda has had its share of violence in the past, most infamously under the bizarre rule of dictatorial Idi Amin, who—besides reputedly using death squads and military forces to kill hundreds of thousands of people—threw all Asians out of the country because he dreamed that God had told him to. He supposedly fed corpses to crocodiles, kept severed heads of opponents in his refrigerator, and enjoyed letting people assume the rumors that he was a cannibal were true. But Amin had been toppled from power in 1979, and for two decades, Uganda had been stabilizing and enjoying economic success. Its only black eye is an ongoing conflict in the northwest, where the Lord's Resistance Army brutally and randomly murders civilians for no apparent reason. The LRA appears to have no agenda, and its actions seem indiscriminate. New LRA soldiers are kidnapped children rather than advocates of any cause.

But the LRA was at the other end of the country from Bwindi, and in 1999, those tourists had no reason to believe that there was danger of anything beyond a sprained ankle incurred during a gorilla trek.

I'd worried more about the safety of going gorilla trekking before September 11. But now, after watching the real danger I might have faced by staying home in New York, the worry of being kidnapped in 2001's Uganda seemed completely unrealistic.

Still, I was relieved when I woke up under my mosquito net in the morning and realized that no rebels had crossed over from Congo during the course of the night. I'd sign the guest book before I left. I'd been overly paranoid.

And my fears were, it turned out, absurdly unfounded. As I walked to the meeting point for the gorilla trek, I spotted glimpses through the trees of Bwindi's "invisible" army of Ugandan soldiers and park rangers. I could hear guns being loaded and men drilling. These men haunted us quietly throughout the day, always beyond view save for a quick glimpse of a rubber boot or tan uniform, but they were never far enough away for us to forget they were there.

At the Uganda Wildlife Authority kiosk at the gate, I joined five other American and European tourists. A uniformed park ranger gave us walking sticks and a briefing. We were due to track Mubare

Group, the original habituated Bwindi gorilla group. Gorillas are habituated through a long process in which researchers and rangers spend time near the gorillas every day, until finally the proximity of nonthreatening humans becomes a nonevent to the foraging gorillas. Six other tourists would spend all day tracking the other gorilla group, which would split a year later into two separate habituated groups.

Luz was our Uganda Wildlife Authority guide. He was accompanied by two trackers, three porters, two armed guards, and one Ugandan university student whose job it was to precisely record everything the gorillas did. Ugandans have great pride and scholarly interest in their gorillas. Gone are the days of indiscriminate poaching and trapping that existed when Dian Fossey first showed up in the volcanic foothills of Rwanda.

We were instructed to follow Luz and the trackers. A ranger gave us an introductory briefing.

"Only six tourists per day can visit each group. The maximum time with each group is one hour. There are no exceptions. *No* flash photography. You must not get closer than five meters. If a gorilla approaches you, back away slowly so there are five meters between you and the gorilla. Always obey your guide."

"Please always be quiet and nonthreatening," said Luz. "You must not wave your arms or move suddenly. If a gorilla charges you, kneel down on all fours and submissively look at the ground."

And pretend to eat grass, I added silently. That was what Dian Fossey had done.

Perhaps the grass-eating had been discredited as overkill,

or perhaps the guides had just gotten tired of being laughed at by tourists. We were sent off gorilla-tracking without these vital instructions. I, for one, would certainly eat grass if it meant not being attacked by an angry gorilla.

Our trackers led us along a dirt track for ten minutes and then took a startling right turn into a dense jungle of mud and green undergrowth.

It was the "impenetrable" bit of Bwindi Impenetrable National Park that should have tipped me off. The rain, mud, and vegetation were impenetrable enough on their own, but the massive slopes complicated the trek. I leaned heavily on my walking stick, poking it into mud and putting all my weight on it as I propelled myself up jungle hills. There was no trail. Trackers with machetes hacked the route out of the bush as we followed the elusive signs of gorilla activity—they'd point out a pile of dung here, a flattened plant there.

I'd been drenched in sweat almost as soon as we entered the forest. It was chilly in the morning mist, but the air was thick with humidity. I was just starting to take short breaths and wishing I'd brought some sort of gardening gloves so I could hang onto vines to help pull myself up, when, after ten minutes, we turned and started to hike back downhill.

We arrived back at the road. Our uphill escapade had been in vain. The trackers followed the gorilla trail to the left of the road this time.

Later, I would suspect that the trackers had deliberately taken us off course to give us a taste of tracking so that we wouldn't feel cheated at having missed our chance to slide around in the mud and humidity. Gorilla-tracking was famed for being arduous and taking all day. We were supposed to have been exhausted from scrambling on all fours through dense vegetation. None of us complained at missing the chance to sweat more in the jungle.

Mubare Group was only fifty feet from the road.

"Leave your sticks," whispered Luz. Gorillas, apparently, don't like humans to carry big sticks. We leaned our sticks against a tree, put down our bags, and got our cameras ready. I'd loaded in 1600-speed film, having heard that it was dark under the canopy of the impenetrable forest.

"Look, he's mating," said Luz.

We all surged forward to see the dominant silverback at work. Dominant male mountain gorillas keep small harems and mate with all the adult females in the group.

"That's it?" I thought. The silverback sat passively, a bored expression on his face.

The flattened female gorilla under him looked more like a gorilla-skin rug than a living mountain gorilla. I'd expected noises or at least movement. Perhaps we'd just seen the end.

We had. The silverback—so named for the silver stripe that adult male mountain gorillas develop—stood up, leaning on his knuckles, and then casually strolled away through the clearing. We were only five meters away from him, but he seemed oblivious to our presence. He was shorter than I'd expected. In my imagination, inspired by too much *King Kong* and *Magilla Gorilla*, I'd expected a hulking giant of a gorilla. But mountain gorillas are short and squat.

Mubare Group's silverback was named "Sleeps-A-Lot." But Sleeps-

A-Lot didn't sleep today. He posed for a bit, taunting me as I realized that even high-speed film was not fast enough for the dark forest. Then he plodded over to the trees, where he effortlessly pulled himself up into the forest canopy and disappeared.

"They are searching for berries," whispered Luz. The Ugandan university student scribbled furiously in his notebook. "Mates. Stands up. Ignores. Climbs."

We couldn't see much of the gorillas, and I was getting anxious. The permit guaranteed us an hour in the presence of the gorillas, but not an hour of viewing the gorillas. If the gorillas chose to stay in the trees for the whole hour, that was their prerogative and our tough luck.

Perhaps, I thought, *we couldn't see the gorillas, but we could certainly hear them.*

"*Fzzzzrrtt!*" The silverback let one fly.

"*Brrrrrzzzt!*" So did the female he'd been squashing earlier.

We spent forty minutes listening to gorilla farts.

"Do they always do that?" I whispered to Luz.

He nodded. "They are vegetarian."

Funny, Dian Fossey never mentioned gorilla gas in her book. Maybe she was so accustomed to it that it didn't merit so much as a mention. Maybe I'd found the gorillas on a particularly flatulent day.

While I listened, I thought with envy of a friend's trip to see the gorillas. He'd seen a mother and newborn. All the female gorillas had been clustered around the newborn, and they were nearly human in the way they'd seemed to have been "oohing" and "aahing" while the silverback sat proudly nearby. I was a little disappointed. My gorilla experience seemed doomed to be an audible one, not a visual one.

Finally, as if on some silent cue, the gorillas descended into the undergrowth. Sleeps-A-Lot was the largest and still looked to be only about half my size, even though he'd probably stretch to five feet if he were trying to make a point. Their funny shapes didn't impede their agility, however. The gorillas—for the most part—gracefully propelled themselves earthward by using branches and vines and thumbs. They seemed to exert no effort at all. A few of the younger ones were less graceful and nearly plummeted to the ground. It was gorgeous to watch, and I forgot about the $250 I'd spent on the permit as the twelve fat little apes descended as one. They began to disappear, one by one, into the dense rainforest bush.

"It's been one hour," said Luz. Reluctantly, we picked up our walking sticks and plowed through the mud back to the road.

It had felt like ten minutes.

Once we were clear of the forest and our primate friends were long gone, our group erupted into chatter.

"Did you see when he climbed up?"

"Did you see when he climbed down?"

"Did you see the baby?"

We could add nothing to the experience by talking about it, but everyone was babbling with excitement. We hadn't even needed the bonding of trekking through the jungle together for hours to become a team; all we needed was the shared moment.

I was dreading tomorrow's bus ride back to Kampala, so as the group walked, I asked around to see if anyone was headed by car across the mountains to the town of Kabale. The road was too steep for a bus, but it was just three hours' drive by private car. From Kabale, a six-hour bus ride along paved roads would get me to Kampala.

"Do you want a lift? We're going to Lake Bunyonyi," said a Spanish man. He and his wife had hired a minivan and driver for their holiday in Uganda.

"Yes, if it's okay with your driver." Lake Bunyonyi has a popular resort and is only a few miles from Kabale.

The Ugandan driver was not only okay with it, but he was an honorable gentleman who took a personal interest in getting me safely to Kabale. He was cautious and slowed down when he saw kids or animals near the road. He gave bicycles and chickens the right-of-way. We drove over the mountain on a dirt road—past agricultural terraces and banana trees, and through the rain and mist—to arrive in town by late afternoon.

"Do you know where you will stay?" asked the driver.

"How about this hotel?" I pointed to a listing in my guidebook. It was a large, European-style hotel but it was the easiest place to find, and rain was pouring steadily. I didn't want to take him out of his way.

He sniffed.

"That is too expensive. I will take you to a good hotel."

He left me at Sky Blue, a basic but friendly spot. The other customers were all African. My room was simple, barely more than a bed and a locking door. But the shared shower across the open courtyard spouted hot water, and after a morning of sweating in the jungle and an afternoon of freezing in the mountain rain, I was thrilled with my accommodation.

I wanted to catch the first bus of the day the next morning, but when I tried to leave at 6 AM, I discovered we were all locked in behind window bars and gates. Submerging my fears about fire hazards, I called to the guard outside, who pointed me to a door that I was to knock on to wake the manager. The manager rolled out of bed, let me out, and then locked the gate behind me.

"Do you know where I catch the bus?" I asked the guard, a bored-looking man in his thirties. Like most Ugandan security guards, he looked eager to chat. He also held a semiautomatic weapon.

"It will come." He spoke slowly. His English was limited. Again, I was faced with having no idea which language he spoke. I did not know which part of my guidebook to look at for the right words to butcher in my attempts to pronounce them.

"Here? Bus?" I pointed to the ground.

He nodded and made a calming, horizontal motion with his hand.

"It will come."

He told me long stories about his life (none of which I understood), while I nodded appreciatively. It appeared that he'd once been a guard at Bwindi. I watched anxiously for the bus. It seemed unlikely that the Kabale bus stop was situated so conveniently in front of my hotel.

Finally, twenty minutes later, the lights of a bus came down the street. The guard walked to the curb and flapped a hand. The bus stopped and I hopped on, waving goodbye to my new friend.

As it turned out, the Kampala-bound bus makes several circuits of Kabale before heading north. We drove up and down the main street for a half hour, slowing to the speed of all pedestrians while the conductor invited them to board (whether they wanted to or not).

Our trip to Kampala was without mishap, aside from one quickly changed flat tire. I arrived in Kampala in time for lunch.

I finished *Gorillas in the Mist* on the bus, concerned when Dian Fossey mentioned her irritation at gorilla tourism. Primates catch human illnesses easily and are stressed by strangers traipsing up to them and snapping photos. They alter their behavioral patterns, and while Luz had made us adhere to strict guidelines set by Uganda Wildlife Authority, it seemed likely that misguided tourists occasionally used camera flashes or beat their chests at the gorillas. Even so, I thought Fossey was wrong to discount gorilla tourism.

In the early '80s, there were 242 mountain gorillas left in the wild. Today there are more than six hundred, spread out over southwestern Uganda, northern Rwanda, and part of the Democratic Republic of Congo. This is surely due to public awareness and gorilla tourism. At $250 a visit (later raised to $360), plus ancillary income from visas, hotels, and transportation, the mountain gorillas were a resource worth protecting.

"Would the mountain gorilla be a species doomed to extinction in the same century in which it was discovered?" Dian Fossey had asked this disheartening question in her book.

The answer, thanks to Dian Fossey's work and gorilla tourism, was no.

Chapter 12

Jambo, I'll Have Your Money Now, OR, A Week in Nairobi

"Jambo."

I was in downtown Nairobi, looking for a travel agent so that I could book a balloon flight over Masai Mara. The man who had said "hello" in Swahili had fallen into step alongside me. He was tall, dressed in casual clothing, and smiled at me with familiarity. My "scam sense" throbbed dully.

"Still walking, huh?"

I didn't know what he was talking about. I'd never seen him before and had been walking for only about ten minutes. I'd just arrived from Kampala and had quickly found a cheap hotel room on the edge of a squalid block of green that passed for parkland.

I'd walked about six blocks from my hotel. That was all. I made a noncommittal noise.

"Hmghph," I replied.

"You don't remember me, do you?" he asked.

Ah, I knew this one. I stifled a giggle.

The remember-me-from-the-hotel scam was documented in my guidebook. The goal was to engage me in conversation, make me think I knew him, and then ask me for a small loan, which would be repaid later at the hotel.

I shook my head.

"John. From the hotel," he said.

"I'm not staying in a hotel," I lied.

"I mean the hostel. You don't recognize me out of my uniform."

"I'm not staying in a hostel." I stared him coolly in the eyes.

He knew I was on to him.

"Son of a bitch," he snarled and strode away. I was too surprised at his anger to correct his English usage. *Bitch* could be applied to me, but *son?*

The same guidebook that tipped me off to the scam stated that Kenya had the third-largest gap between rich and poor in the world. Many travelers jokingly referred to Nairobi as "Nairobbery," and stories told in hostels around Africa were rife with warnings.

"I was with two other large men, and we left the hotel to get dinner. We had just stepped outside the front door, when a man ran up out of nowhere. He reached over, still running, and grabbed the shirt pocket of the Australian I was with—and kept running, ripping off the pocket and taking it away with him."

This story was told to me over a hostel dinner in Zambia by a British rugby coach. He was a big guy.

"The Australian didn't have anything in his pocket, but he could have. We all three turned right around and went back into the hotel. You have to take the warnings about Nairobi seriously."

Paranoia was already on my mind when the hotel staff issued me several warnings at check-in.

"Madam, you must never carry a bag in Nairobi. You may put things in your pockets but you must not carry a bag. They will cut the strap and take the bag."

"You must not wear expensive sunglasses. They will grab them right off your head."

"You must always take a taxi after dark."

Blah, blah, blah. Enough already! I had heard so many warnings that I had become skeptical. Nairobi had at least one and a half million people living in it, and they wouldn't live there if they were mugged three times a day.

Besides, I'd been told the same thing about carrying bags in Windhoek, and the same thing about sunglasses in Victoria Falls. Of course I'd take the warnings seriously, but not so seriously as to be frozen into place, afraid to leave my hotel. And my bag already had a slash in it, from Mongolia. A group of men had surrounded me in a department store entrance, crowding me while one slashed my bag. I had instinctively pushed them away and moved on, not noticing the tear in the bag until I put it down by the computer in the cybercafé and watched the contents spill out onto the mousepad. Nairobi, I'd later discover, was a good place to get the canvas repaired.

I continued toward the travel agency, fending off children asking for contributions to their school programs and young men touting for souvenir shops.

"*Jambo!* Where are you from?" I was asked this a half dozen times. It was always a prelude to "Come to my shop." It was a Friday afternoon and businesses would close soon. I didn't have time to browse. And the answer "New York" or "U.S.A." just made the touts more relentless. The dollar was strong and Americans on holiday were known to spend. How could the touts know that I was traveling for a year on pocket lint?

"New Zealand," I'd reply. Maybe they'd know the Kiwi dollar was weak.

"I'm going there to university next year!" I couldn't outwit these guys. This line was a scam too. There'd be a long discussion in which it would be revealed that the tout was miraculously attending college in the town I was from, and then somehow money would get involved. I didn't hang around long enough to get the details. I muttered something about sheep and bolted.

Another man tried to sell me a basket.

"American?" He asked cheerfully.

"Maybe." I replied, briskly walking away before he could take the conversation further.

"Taliban," he hissed after me.

When I found the travel agent twenty minutes later—a straightforward young woman sitting in an upstairs office at a desk littered with brochures—it turned out that she did have a way to get me onto a balloon over Masai Mara. I had doubts. It would cost me $400. I was paying $13 for a Nairobi hotel room, dodging small children begging for school fees, and giving coins to the woman and three children who lived on the sidewalk by my hotel.

"You can go tomorrow with one safari, stay overnight in a tent at Maasai Camp, go on the balloon safari on Sunday morning, and you can return Sunday afternoon with a different safari."

I agonized. That was a *lot* of money. I'd seen plenty of animals already, had gone on several safaris throughout Africa, and had traveled through the Serengeti, which was basically the same as Masai Mara but across the border. But I'd never ridden in a balloon. The MariesWorldTour.com readers were for it, voting overwhelmingly for me to forget the cost and go for the experience. Their instructions were clear: Climb every mountain, take every balloon, personally introduce self to every baboon and gorilla, and watch out for bad guys.

But too many times I had fallen for the once-in-a-lifetime appeal of something. Only a few days ago, I'd forked over several hundred dollars to spend an hour listening to farting mountain gorillas. *Was this priceless too or would I kick myself later? Would this be something to tell my grandchildren about? Would I even have grandchildren since I couldn't seem to stay in one place long enough to eat dinner with the same man twice?*

My gut—which wasn't paying for the ride—said "yes" to the balloon. I put the balloon trip on my credit card. The agent buzzed me out of the gate guarding the door of the tiny office, and I tripped down the steps to the sidewalk, compartmentalizing my guilt as I dodged touts on the street.

"Madam, balloon?" whispered a blanket-clad Maasai warrior from outside my tent in the Mara two mornings later. I opened my eyes. It was 4:20 AM.

"Yes, I'm awake." My immediate neighbors were probably awake as well, cursing me for my early-morning wake-up call by the selfless Maasai.

"Shower?"

I unzipped the door, thinking how loud a zipper sounded in a soundless night.

"Yes. I'd like a shower."

He held out a bucket of water.

An hour later, a British balloon pilot named John turned up the blue and orange gas flame as our balloon rose over the Rift Valley. I was in a basket with a friendly young blond couple from San Diego, and we marveled together at the yellow-green plains recently cropped short by migrating wildebeests. We saw rhinos, gazelles, impalas, and a few giraffes. The pilot told us not only about details of the animal kingdom, but also that he'd once piloted Michael Palin along the same route.

The day brightened but unfortunately only to a dull gray. Rain drizzled intermittently. The animals did not turn out en masse to visit with us. Disappointed when we set down sixty-five minutes after we'd taken off, I reminded myself that the balloon company could not control the weather or the wildlife. The basket tipped over as we landed. Helpers guided the orange and yellow balloon over onto its side and let it deflate.

Our ride had taken just more than an hour. The next hour of our two-hour balloon ride was spent eating a simple brunch, while the balloon company tried to sell us souvenirs.

At $400 a head, I thought, *they should be giving us souvenirs.*

But I couldn't complain. I had known in advance that the price was more unforgettable than the trip and had deliberately overlooked the cost. I'd been in a balloon over Masai Mara now. I wouldn't need to do it again.

Two cups of coffee and a croissant later, I joined an Australian family in an old minivan for the ride out of Rift Valley. The driver never slowed down for puddles on the dirt road, preferring to take the unknown at top speed. We kept getting stuck and then having to wait while the distributor dried out. After the first few interludes, even the three children yelled, "Drive around it," as we approached each puddle. We passed several Land Rovers that were off-track, practically chasing animals, which was highly illegal. We made slow progress as we climbed for several hours toward the highway to Nairobi.

As I learned to navigate the streets of Nairobi, I became subjected less frequently to potential scams in Kenya's main city. I walked with confidence and learned to take buses and *matatus*. I drank coffee and had breakfast with Maasai men in the hotel restaurant. Many of them wore city clothes when they visited Nairobi, their stretched earlobes and beaded earrings giving away that they were not quite the average office worker in this urban landscape. They stared alongside me at CNN as the first U.S. bombs dropped on Afghanistan. No one speculated. We all watched in silence.

Breakfast was included in my hotel cost, but nothing else in Nairobi was free. As in many cities I'd visited in Africa, there were multiple parallel economies. To me, Nairobi was expensive for a cheap city. As a short-term visitor, I was not privy to the local economy, and anything imported or geared toward expats or tourists had a correspondingly inflated price tag. At a shopping center in suburban Westlands, a fashionable Kenyan man with dreadlocks made me a blonde again while laughing at the price the Hilton hair salon had quoted me. The Hilton salon wanted $70 just to lighten my roots. I wouldn't pay that even at home, I told him. Just like at home, services in the upscale hotels were pricier than in the suburban shops geared toward the masses.

I'd gone to see my hairdresser in New York before I'd left, to ask if she thought I should return to my natural light brown.

"That takes maintenance too," she'd replied. "You'll have better luck finding people who can lighten your hair than people who can match a tone as it washes out."

I'd had good luck in Australia, Singapore, and Hong Kong. But my faux blond color had become erratic after Central Asia, and I could now tell where I'd been by the bands of blond across my hair. The lightest was from Estonia, the darkest from Cape Town. The orange was courtesy of a sweet Indian woman in Dar Es Salaam. It would take years to make it all one color again, but the fun of sitting with local women in salons around the world, listening to them chat and watching them get their nails done, was irreplaceable.

My Westlands hairdresser said he was surprised that the Hilton colorist hadn't invited me to her home to do my hair privately at a steep discount. Everyone in Nairobi seemed to have an innovative way of making money on the side. And thus began my education in how people make a living in Nairobi.

When I went to buy a small lightweight tent the next day, the salesman said that the shop was sold out of tents, but he could get me a used one at a good price. I agreed to what sounded like a reasonable deal. I watched as he filled out some forms and I realized that he was officially "renting" me a tent. The deposit more than paid for the tent.

"I'm not returning this," I said with alarm.

"Of course not." The salesman looked as me as if I were a fool. He then charged me an additional fee—that surely went straight into his pocket—to sew up the small holes in the tent's nylon and to fill out the rental forms correctly.

Then, the salesman at a souvenir shop finished my education in Nairobi's economy. I had been hunting for a specific type of Congolese textile as a souvenir for Turbo, the Australian bug-eating champion I'd met in China. The only one I'd seen to date had been under glass at the Dar Es Salaam Sheraton. Now, the ones I found in the African gallery were $35 each.

'That's too much," I told the salesman. That didn't stop him. Later, he met me at an Internet café and sold me the textiles at half price. He said he'd gotten them directly from the supplier and bypassed the shop. But years later, a friend suggested a more likely scenario that made me feel both ashamed for having encouraged it and completely naive for having not caught on and sending the salesman away.

"He probably stole them from the shop, you know."

Out in Westlands, an outdoor artisans market sits across from Sarit Centre, behind the mall where I'd gotten my hair colored. I headed there the next day to hunt among the souvenir stands for wooden hippos, as a friend in California collects all things hippopotamus. Word had spread like wildfire that I was looking at hippos and everyone waved forearm-size hippos at me from their booths.

"Where are you from?" asked a would-be hippo salesman.

"New York," I said.

He clucked and shook his head.

"Osama was very bad," said the seller with a smile, as if his personal friend Osama bin Laden were a naughty boy who needed to be put in a corner.

At the next table, an Arabic-Kenyan shopkeeper told me simply, "They need to kill him." I didn't buy a hippo from him either, though I did buy a foot-long blond wooden hippo from an artisan in Nakuru later in the week.

I walked to the nearby Sarit Centre, where two Kenyan men in long-sleeved button-up shirts were giving away puppies. They were standing at the car entrance next to a cardboard box, and each man was holding two puppies. The puppies, black and brown blotched mutts with tan eyebrows, looked barely larger than the wooden hippos I'd just looked at. I happily borrowed the puppies and cuddled them, but I had to return them for the heartbreaking walk away. The men spoke no English, and they had no idea what I meant when I explained why I couldn't possibly take the little dogs.

"I am sorry. They are very cute. Puppies very cute. But I do not live here. I go to United States. New York. *Zoom*. No puppies." I pointed to myself and then made a plane motion with my hands. Of course I was taking an ocean liner across the Atlantic, but this was not the time for details.

I noticed a dermatologist's office on the top floor of the Sarit Centre, so I dropped by to see what she made of the hard swollen lump on my upper left arm. It had appeared right after I'd gotten my second rabies vaccine in Berlin, and it definitely didn't belong there. It was the size of a large mosquito bite, the kind that had been picked at for days, but it didn't itch. I had tried ignoring the lump, but it hadn't disappeared on its own.

"Keep an eye on it," were the dermatologist's instructions.

I didn't want to keep an eye on it. I wanted it gone. I picked and scratched at it for several more weeks until an Ethiopian doctor finally gave me a tube of goo that vanquished the lump within days.

The *matatu* that took me back downtown from the Sarit Centre was blasting Kenyan rap through its bass-heavy speakers. The African rap sounded unsophisticated to my American ears. *How funny that the African influence on American pop culture had come full circle to where American culture was as influential in Africa as Africa had been, in turn, on America.*

One passenger in the *matatu* asked the conductor for change. The conductor checked his pockets. He didn't have any. He asked each passenger, in either Swahili or English depending on the appearance of the passenger, for change. No one had change.

The driver stopped the *matatu* at a traffic backup. The conductor slid the passenger door open and ran to the taxi behind us to get change. We drove slowly on through the traffic.

Looking back, I could see that the conductor had noticed we were moving, but, was still waiting, his hand out by the taxi window. He looked up and at us disappearing into the distance and then back to the taxi window.

He finally got his change and took off at a run. But the traffic had lessened and we were driving rapidly. *Surely the driver had seen the conductor leave the minivan?*

He hadn't. One of the passengers spoke sharply in Swahili. The driver glanced into his rear-view mirror and stopped immediately. The conductor ran up and leaped into the *matatu,* laughing as he caught his breath.

On my last scheduled night in Nairobi, I had dinner with Howard and Sonia, an expat couple who were friends of a friend. Their home, car, children, and furnishings were all high quality and gorgeous. Their kids attended an American school and had all the conveniences of life at home, but they appeared insulated from the junk food and targeted marketing at kids back in the States. Maybe the expat lifestyle had a lot to offer families. We had dinner at a Thai restaurant, and they dropped me off back at my hotel.

"That's the terrorist hotel!" Sonia said. The terrorists who had bombed the U.S. Embassy had stayed at my hotel. I hoped they hadn't stayed in room 407.

At ten on Thursday morning, I headed to the 680 Hotel on Kenyatta Avenue. I'd eaten delicious Japanese food around the corner from there two days ago, but this time I was going to meet a group on the hotel terrace.

Dragoman, an overland-truck company, was going to take me north through Lake Turkana and Ethiopia. I had bought, rather, "rented," my tent and brought along a Therm-a-Rest solely for the camping on this trip.

"PAZ," a smallish white truck with the standard-issue Dragoman orange stripe and DISCOVER THE DREAM slogan painted on its side, sat in front of the 680. I'd been crossing paths with PAZ ever since Namibia, and I was surprised that it was going to be my home for the next month and a half.

Inside the 680, two men sat on the terrace. They were both tall and slightly unkempt, with sun-worn faces, sandy-blond hair, and clean but old clothing. To me, their appearances screamed "overland truck drivers." They were wearing normal clothes instead of the safari gear that so many tourists show up in, but more importantly, they looked at ease instead of nervous, as they would be if they were fresh off the plane. I sat down and introduced myself.

Mark, the taller one with short hair, a cigarette, and a gin and tonic in his hand, was the leader. He was Dragoman's Ethiopia expert and, at 37, had been Drago-driving for more than eight years.

Tony, a former scientist with chest-length hair and glasses, was codriving. He was equally capable and had been driving Dragoman trucks for four or five years.

But the real surprise was that we were going to have a cook on board.

Wow! What a luxury! Presumably this meant I wouldn't be subjected to tuna surprise or peanut butter sandwiches twice a day.

The group for the Nairobi-to–Addis Ababa leg consisted of ten tourists—one German man, three men and five women from the United Kingdom/Ireland, and me. Six had been together for weeks already and it showed. They were cliquish and insular. Very few of the experienced overlanders seemed interested in the new arrivals. *Never mind,* I thought. *Typical behavior for a group that's been traveling together for weeks.*

We'd all get to know each other with time, and by the time we got new people in Addis, we'd look equally cliquish to them.

Monica, a thirty-one-year-old Scot with curly dark hair and a laughing smile, was my assigned roommate. She'd lived in Norway and Azerbaijan in her work as a surveyor. Lucky Monica would get her own tent, but we'd share when the group stayed in hotels.

Monica filled me in right away on yet another Nairobi scam, one that I had somehow missed out on.

A man on the street had engaged her in conversation while she'd been souvenir-hunting. After a minute, she'd managed to extricate herself and move on. Then a second man approached her, claiming to be an undercover policeman. He was investigating the man she'd just spoken to, and would she mind coming with him? Sensible Monica had refused to get in the "policeman's" car and suggested they first discuss the matter with a nearby uniformed policeman. The undercover "policeman" then let the matter drop and vanished.

My new group, I told Mark, was going to have start without me. I'd spent too much time looking at mountain gorillas and flying above Masai Mara and had fallen behind on my Web duties. I begged off Elsamere and Hell's Gate National Park—*Born Free* could live on without my visit. Mark agreed and suggested I catch up with the group on Sunday in the town of Nakuru.

The group started the trip without me, and I slaved away in the Internet café for two solid days. The taxi drivers began to surprise me by saying the name of my hotel before I opened my mouth. Waitresses started to greet me on the street.

On the second day, I was startled to see a Dragoman truck outside the 680. But it wasn't PAZ. It was Oscar, identified by the OAZ on its license plate.

In '98, Oscar was the large, then-new truck that had carried me from Kathmandu to Damascus. Nikki had driven, while Paul (whom I'd recently met up with in Arusha) had codriven.

A driver was climbing out of Oscar.

"Excuse me," I said. He looked at me apprehensively.

"Is this truck Oscar?" I asked.

"Yeah . . ." The driver started to smile.

"This truck took me through the Middle East," I explained. "He's had a few modifications since then."

This Oscar was older and more distinguished. He had a wood rack added to his back, a padlock on the driver's door, and had the word OSCAR written on his side in Ethiopian Amharic.

"It's the Ethiopia truck," said the driver. "But Oscar is sick so he has to be shipped back to the U.K. from Durban."

What a pity. I quite liked the idea that my old friend Oscar would take me through Ethiopia. Plus, Oscar was a lot bigger than PAZ.

I left 680 and walked for a coffee. I wasn't ready to leave Nairobi yet. I was just getting comfortable with it. I was getting used to the smell of the city where it was easy to buy deodorant but harder to find antiperspirant. People were just starting to recognize and greet me. But the Dragoman truck was heading north to Ethiopia, and if I missed it, I'd have to hitch a ride on a desert cargo truck. Despite my wariness of group activities, I knew I had to go with Dragoman. I headed toward the hotel to pack my bag. A familiar man, the same man who had called me a "son of a bitch" earlier in the week, walked up beside me.

"Still walking, huh?"

"You already tried this once," I responded, smiling.

"Son of a bitch," he said and strode away.

Chapter 13

Where the Pavement Ends

Why on earth did I think I could deal with an organized trip? I wondered as the Dragoman overland truck I had boarded lurched over a pothole and out of the Kenyan town of Nakuru. The preponderance of evidence suggested that I was deficient in team spirit.

The nine other tourists on board had done a lot of moving in while they'd been traveling together, whereas I'd run errands in Nairobi for the last three days, and several of them had been together for two months on the way up from Cape Town. They sat stone-faced as I boarded and walked down the aisle, looking for an empty seat. There were few, as most were filled with possessions, the international sign of "Leave me alone and don't sit next to me."

I sat in the back with Monica and Charles, the other two newcomers who had joined the truck in Nairobi. I smiled gratefully at their welcoming expressions and then stared out the window at the grassy roadside. I was grumpy, already experiencing a sensation not unlike claustrophobia. And I was tired. I'd woken early in Nairobi to rendezvous with the truck on time.

The taxi drivers lounging outside my hotel initially had ignored me that morning. For days, they'd approached me right after breakfast to query hopefully: "Taxi?" Every day I would smile, shake my head, and then walk to the bus stop.

I was perplexed when no one offered me a ride that day. Perhaps they'd gotten tired of rejection. I stared at the drivers, wondering why they continued to chat among themselves.

"Taxi?" one finally asked after staring back at me for a minute. He shifted his gaze onto the massive backpack I was wearing.

"Yes," I replied. "Please take me to the Peugeots to Nakuru."

"Nakuru? You want to go to Nakuru?"

"Yes."

He asked his friend a few questions in Swahili. The friend answered rapidly while motioning, obviously explaining the location of the Nakuru transport.

"Pehjet or Neeson?" asked the taxi driver. He had not understood my request for a Peugeot.

"Pehjet," I responded.

"Ah, Pehjet! Let's go."

We drove to Cross Road, a bumpy frontierlike dirt road near where I'd caught the Busscar coach to Uganda. The driver left me at "Cross Road Travel," and I put my bag into a Pehjet that had a NAKURU sign on its windshield. A man with a badge escorted me to the ticket window.

"This is my friend," declared the man, pointing to me. "Please give her a good seat to Nakuru." The ticket seller laughed and sold me a seat for 300 shillings. My new pal took me back to the Peugeot and motioned me into the front passenger-side seat—the best seat in the car, as long as the seatbelts worked and you didn't plow into any stray animals.

I sat in place for an hour, while the driver washed the car and waited for the other seven seats to fill up. We left just before nine thirty. I was to meet my group at eleven thirty at a Nakuru hotel and was a bit concerned.

But I needn't have worried. Peugeot drivers are famous for speeding recklessly, and we zipped past cars, roadside baboons, and trucks before pulling into Nakuru at eleven forty. The Dragoman truck showed up at the meeting point ten minutes after I did.

Now, after rejoining Monica and Charles and contemplating my lack of team spirit, I settled in for a nap as PAZ drove on. But I was thwarted. Shortly after leaving Nakuru, the truck pulled over at a tall yellow sign that had a hand-painted shape of Africa on it. EQUATOR was stenciled across a white band bisecting the center. Below that were the words JAMBO KENYA.

The nine other tourists and I piled out of the truck by climbing down the steel ladder. We toted our cameras along for obligatory "Here I am at the equator" shots. I got a better look at the group I'd be traveling with on and off for the next month. We all wore the uniform of the African overland tourist: sunglasses, shorts, sandals, and T-shirts. Pith helmets and safari vests are, of course, the stuff of myth.

Villagers walked nearby, but they ignored us. A truckload of tourists taking photos at the equator was a common sight. Then a man in a purple polo shirt and baseball cap appeared, carrying a bottle of water, a jug, and a bowl with a hole in the middle.

Cool, I thought. It was time for the famous water-draining-the-wrong-way trick! I'd get to see the famous huckster gimmick up close. The other passengers were somewhat interested too. *Did it really work? Was it a scam?*

People who have seen the water drain in different directions swear that it really happens. They've seen it with their own eyes. The reason they've seen it happen is because it does happen. Water does sometimes drain in different directions on opposite sides of the equator. And the beauty of this cool effect is that you can replicate it in the privacy of your own home—even when solidly ensconced in one hemisphere or another—with a little skill and practice.

Our day's drive ended at Thomson's Falls in Nyahururu, where I assembled the little blue tent I'd "rented" in Nairobi, to the mockery of all.

"That's yours?" said Mark. "I thought it was a children's tent."

It probably was. When Mark lay down in it to make his point, his feet stuck out the end. Fortunately, I was a good deal smaller than Mark and the tent was just my size.

Dragoman supplied its clients with sturdy, canvas two-person tents. But I didn't want to share a tent with a stranger. I wanted to be able to roll over without waking someone else up, to get up when

I felt like getting up without guilt over waking up too early, and to have the freedom of being able to go to bed when I pleased without worrying about someone else's schedule.

I had a cold drink with the group, and as the others talked and laughed as people do, about shared experiences but also about what I'd been doing in Africa, it slowly dawned on me that I was the one with the chip on my shoulder. The individual group members were pleasant enough, and they seemed happy to have a new face in their group, in spite of not wanting that face next to them on the truck.

After we hiked down to the falls, the rest of the group went to the bar. I'd had enough group interaction for one day, so I took a cold shower in a shack and then retired to the solitary privacy of the little blue tent. I curled up in my sleeping bag and fleece sleep-sheet, on my own camping mat that I'd carried all the way from Europe, and read by the light of a candle I had placed on the dirt outside the entrance. The sound of crickets, the splash of the falls, and the hum of a distant generator lulled me to sleep.

The next day took us first through Isiolo—the last outpost of paved road, Internet access, and chocolate for two weeks' time—until arrival at Addis Ababa. From here on in, the roads would be dusty, potholed, and uncomfortable.

I could have gotten this far on my own in a Peugeot, but after this I would have had to stick my thumb out. Other travelers had made it through the Isiolo-to-Ethiopia section on the backs of cattle trucks, clinging to the bars over the cows and hoping not to get shot at by bandits.

Today's destination was Samburu National Park. The hot drive took us through the game reserve, past animals on the way to our campsite by Samburu Lodge.

The most unusual animal was Grevy's zebra, a large, psychedelic, enhanced zebra found only in this region. The other zebras I had seen south of Kenya were smaller and had wider stripes. We stared at the zebras. They stopped drinking and stared back at us.

"Did you know that a zebra cross-bred with a horse produces a zorse?" asked someone.

No, I hadn't.

Other than zebras, we saw only a few giraffes and a pair of dik-diks, nearly obscured by a scrubby bush.

After setting up our tents, we walked over to Samburu Lodge to watch leopard-baiting. The lodge employees hang a piece of meat in a clearing every night, and sometimes a leopard comes to snack on it.

But not tonight. The leopard must not have been hungry. I wasn't sure whether or not to be disappointed, as leopard-baiting seemed a questionable practice. An alert ranger with a gun accompanied us on our walk back to our campsite, in case the leopard did show up looking for a snack.

The wind came up while we were sleeping, and when it calmed down, I awoke to hear an animal outside my tent. I heard the faint crackling of feet on undergrowth, practically next to my head. It stopped. Then, quiet. It started again, the faintest shuffling.

I'm going to be eaten by a lion, I thought. *My tent is too lightweight and doesn't stink of canvas. The lion will smell me, a Marie-snack waiting to be eaten, like a hot dog wrapped in a tent instead of a bun! What a stupid way to go, eaten by a lion because I was too grumpy to share a canvas tent.*

I lay paralyzed with fear for what was probably minutes but seemed like hours. Finally the lion went away. I didn't get a lot of sleep after that.

In the morning, I unzipped my tent fly and looked at the tracks outside. They were tiny, heart-shaped, and cloven. I appeared to have been terrorized not by a lion but by a dik-dik.

"It was a killer dik-dik," I declared later when explaining my fear to the group.

Our early-morning game drive netted only two oryx, one kori bustard bird, three giraffes, and a lot of dust. I fell asleep in my seat, having been kept up half the night by the vicious dik-dik.

Our trip to Samburu National Park had been disappointing on the wildlife front, but we still had a tribal visit ahead of us. We left the park and headed to a nearby Samburu village. The Samburu are nomadic herders who live in northern Kenya. They stretch their earlobes, jump when dancing, and wear blankets like their distant relatives the Maasai, but they lean more toward glamorous fashions. The Samburu sometimes color their hair and wear more vibrant jewelry, or even feathers.

We set up our tents at the village campsite and then Steven, the tribal chief, came to visit.

Steven's wardrobe demonstrated a hodgepodge of influences. His earlobes were stretched and pierced in the local tradition. A tribal blanket snugly clung to his waist.

His shirt was a khaki safari vest, embroidered with Canadian flags. He was drinking a can of beer as he greeted us.

"That's nothing," Mark said later, laughing. "He used to show up in these glittery millennium sunglasses that were shaped like a big 2000."

Steven was a true-life real-world hybrid tribesman, a conglomeration of his nomadic lifestyle and the MTV generation. He lived in a hut with no running water or electricity, but he wore millennium sunglasses.

Mark told us a story of how his groups used to visit another nomadic tribe. The tourists were always disappointed by the T-shirts and jeans the locals wore, so the nomads had taken to changing into traditional clothing exclusively for the tourists.

"It got to the point where I was calling them on their mobiles to say, 'Take off your shorts and T-shirts because I'm bringing tourists by,'" Mark said.

Fortunately, someone from Dragoman had found Steven's Samburu village. The village women had organized their village into a cultural center, where they ran a campsite and invited tourists to observe their lifestyles. They were a proud tribe and—Steven's quirky wardrobe aside—had preserved their traditional ways.

What they had adopted from the West—the use of currency, souvenir selling, and canned drinks—had been incorporated into their lifestyle but had not co-opted it. And they ran their cultural center without the haphazard desperation for money seen in some areas.

Steven brought us some bad news.

"You cannot see our village today. All the women have gone to a funeral."

There was no arguing with his flawless logic, so we scheduled our visit for early the next morning and spent the day lazing by the river.

"Is it safe to swim here?" we asked Steven.

"Yes, but there are crocodiles."

"Many crocodiles?"

"Yes."

No one went swimming. And it was a good thing. The next morning we discovered that a lot of the proceeds from the village visits funded the schooling of orphans who had lost their parents to malaria—or crocodiles.

Bored with the lazy afternoon, I wished I could wander anonymously through the streets of Nairobi or Dar. I wanted to do my laundry. But I was hostage to the whims of others as well as to overall inconvenience. I'd need to first borrow a key from another passenger, then find a washbowl in the plastic bins, then unpack the luggage locker, pull out my clothes, and then repack the luggage locker. Showering would also require unpacking the luggage locker as would putting up my tent for a nap. Perhaps I could just read my book—if it weren't locked in the truck, along with my water. Now I remembered that I hated traveling this way, and why I preferred the solitary life of just me and my bag.

Later that night, the Samburu—the women having returned from the funeral—came by to show us traditional song and dance around the campfire. They all shook our hands heartily and accepted beer and cigarettes, but not our strange food.

As they danced, Steven gave us a blow-by-blow interpretation of each song.

"This is the welcome song," he'd say, or "This is the marriage song." The songs all seemed to consist of humming and chanting accented by men's leaping or by women's jerking their shoulders in a startling manner.

What impressed me more than the performances themselves was that the Samburu all worked together, performing not for individual gain but for the Dragoman payment that went to the entire village's community fund, which would be used for education, orphans, or group projects.

After the entertainers left, most of the group chatted and gossiped about people they'd met on earlier legs of their trip together. They'd been on what had been proclaimed the "Love Truck," and the passengers had behaved like drunken rabbits. This horrified me but even worse, most seemed to think this had been an enjoyable experience. I made a beeline for the safety of the little blue tent and noticed that Monica had erected her tent near mine on the antisocial outskirts of the campsite.

In the morning, we headed back to the Samburu village. En route, Monica pointed out footprints in the dirt, footprints that bore the "Michelin" and "Firestone" insignias. Our Samburu friends had sandals that were made of recycled tires.

After more tribal welcome dances and an explanation of which women were married and which were unmarried (as demonstrated by their jewelry), the men demonstrated how to make a fire without matches, though it seemed to take a great deal of effort.

Steven brought us into his mud hut, where we sat on our haunches to admire the sacks of aid food labeled "USA."

The tiny huts were cool in the desert heat because of their small windows and near-darkness. The huts were too small for more than two people, but fortunately, given that Samburu are polygamists, tradition dictated that in a polygamous marriage, each wife would have her own hut. Steven expressed concern that because he was a chief, tradition might force him to take a second wife.

"One wife," he explained, "is enough."

The nearby Catholic mission processed the village members' funds for them, so we were encouraged to buy souvenirs—in any currency. One of our group bought some intricately beaded collars to hang on his wall at home. I contented myself with browsing—there was no hard sell here and anything I bought would have to be carried on my back when I left the truck.

We left the village to start what would soon become a daily routine for us—driving for a long, hot day and then setting up camp in a remote area.

Today's drive took us to a campsite near Maralal. I rented a $4-a-night *banda*—a cabin with a private bathroom—did my laundry, and rinsed the mud off the bottom of the little blue tent. The group was having drinks in the bar and in an uncharacteristic social moment spurred by guilt at my lack of team spirit, I decided to join them.

Then, suddenly and inexplicably, I was having fun and enjoying their company.

Monica, Trigger, and Charles chatted about the redeeming qualities of Teletubbies. Mark and Sam, the cook for this trip, dropped by to discuss Kenyan politics and their own backgrounds.

Sam was vague with details, but he seemed to have a family, farm, and dog somewhere in southern Kenya. He'd gone to seek his fortune in Nairobi. He'd found work there painting trucks and doing odd jobs. He'd met Mark, who had noticed his sharpness and reliability and gotten him work as a Dragoman cook as soon as Dragoman had introduced the cook feature on its African trips. Sam would continue to cook for the next five years, as Dragoman's longest-running African cook, long after Mark had given up the road and moved to Jinja to work for a rafting company.

Mark and his childhood friend Dave—who had also been a Dragoman driver—had both changed their lives after reading a book about a solo motorcyclist who'd ridden around the world.

"Dave gave me a copy of *Jupiter's Travels* once and said when I was done reading it, he had a question for me," explained Mark. "That question was, 'When do we leave?'"

They'd saved money for a few years and then left the south of England to ride motorcycles around Africa and Europe together. Later, they'd both become overland truck drivers at a time when adventure travel was still in its infancy, before marketing departments were hired to bring in tourists who had schedules to adhere to and jobs to return to. Overlanding had been too adventure-driven to adhere to schedules. Mark's first training trip—across Congo—had fallen eight days behind, and he'd been sent ahead by public transport to reschedule flights.

I returned happy to my *banda*. My antigroup hysteria had evaporated for the moment. Maybe the little blue tent and I would make it to Ethiopia after all.

Within a few days, I was used to our daily routine. We'd rise early, breakfast, break down camp, lurch from side to side at twenty kilometers an hour along terrible roads until lunchtime, have a picnic, and then lurch along until it was time to stop and camp again. Once, we stopped for a ride around the local area on camelback, but it hadn't worked out as planned after it became apparent that our tribal guides were leading us around in circles to view the same goats over and over again. One of the camels had bitten Charles twice before we'd called a hasty end to the trek.

When we'd camp—Monica and I still far away from the pack— curious villagers would come to stare at us.

You get used to being stared at in rural areas. I'd had the same experience in India and all over Africa. Remote tribespeople don't have televisions, so they will watch for hours as you do the most mundane, boring things. Watching us dry plates by flapping them, for example, was apparently fascinating.

Eventually, the locals would go home to their own dinners. We'd be left alone with our armed campsite guard.

One night, our guard had taken the pay Mark had given him and bought some alcohol, which he apparently had consumed rapidly as he was now quite intoxicated.

"We have a bit of a situation here," said Mark. He, Tony, and Sam went off to deal with it, leaving us alone to contemplate the dangers of having a drunken armed guard. We watched them, in tense silence, as they walked away, then exploded into a flurry of nervous speculation. Would the situation get worse? Did the guard indeed have a gun?

The "guard" returned his pay sheepishly and wandered off to search out a nice ditch for a nap. Mark hired a new guard, who armed himself with a bow and arrow.

Morning chatter, in Swahili, woke me up. The villagers who

had stared at us so intently had returned, and this time they'd brought souvenirs.

Unfortunately for them, we had no major shoppers in our ranks, and we all chose to ignore the impromptu market, opting instead to eat Sam's delicious french toast and disassemble tents.

I sliced bananas onto my french toast and gobbled it up quickly, praising it loudly to encourage Sam to cook it more often (later I discovered his secret was to spoon in a few heaping tablespoons of sugar into the egg batter). I washed and rinsed my dish, and then I flapped it dry.

". . . eight, nine, ten, eleven, twelve . . ." I stopped flapping and the counting stopped. I resumed flapping. The counting began again.

". . . thirteen, fourteen . . ."

Some village children were practicing their English numbers by counting my flaps. They dissolved into giggles when I spotted them.

We drove on, having to admit that the counting children and the souvenir sellers were pretty much the only Africans we were meeting at the moment. Everything we saw was exposed to harsh sun and covered in a film of grit. All the passengers were going a bit stir-crazy, to the point where opening a can of Spam for lunch became incredibly entertaining, but unfortunately northern Kenya features vast expanses of road between its interesting sights, so there was no way around it.

For miles, we drove slowly over rough gravel road, through the desert's volcanic rock. Eventually, the track turned to dirt as the brilliant green "jade sea" water of Lake Turkana slowly appeared out of the dry, brown and yellow desert. The road wound down to a palm-filled oasis.

Our campground, on the edge of Loyangalani, was a fenced-in tree-filled patch of green with a warm swimming pool. The showers were the usual elevated spouts, but they were enclosed in atmospheric thatched huts.

After a swim, we dried off and took a walk through Loyangalani's village outskirts.

The villagers lived in round dried-palm huts. The various colorful beads worn by the gaunt village women denoted their marital status, while the single strands of white beads were worn only by widows.

We left the parched landscape of the huts behind us and walked back to camp, where our local guide invited us to a disco.

"It isn't really a disco," he explained. "It's a dance put on by some local guys. It's in the school."

This sounded as if it could be either awful or intriguing. Charles and I followed the guide to the school. I peeked in through the window.

"Hello!" Three men hung their heads out and gaped at me. Startled, I drew back. They drew closer. I fled for the others, who had walked around to the front door to stare into the school.

There were about thirty men inside, all horsing around while music played.

"Are there any women?" I asked our guide.

He went in to check. He returned a few minutes later.

"There are two in the corner," he pronounced with satisfaction.

"I'm not going in there," I said. Charles was equally unwilling to go. We walked back to camp under the dark palm trees that swayed with the wind.

I crawled into my tent and turned off my flashlight. I zipped open the little blue tent's fly and stared up at the night sky. It was brilliant with clear stars, and the sound of frogs was just audible over the wind. The days were long and the drives suffocating, but the night skies were worth the discomfort.

Chapter 14

The Dire Effects of Salt-Pan Syndrome

"Remarkable in its tedium," I wrote in my diary during the long, hot drive from Loyangalani to Kalacha. There was nothing to see at Kalacha—it was just a necessary overnight camping stop on the way to Marsabit, which was itself a dusty frontier stopover between Lake Turkana and the Ethiopian border. These were driving days, and we passengers sat quietly, numb from boredom. An occasional joke broke the silence, but sitting in a hot, moving vehicle in the Kenyan desert was much like sitting in a hot, moving vehicle anywhere in the world. I read my guidebook. I stared out the window at the rocky lunaresque landscape we were driving across.

Once, the truck lurched to an unexpected halt. We were stuck in gravel. Everyone piled out to watch the crew simply and easily dig the truck out, using a shovel and sand mats. They dug the rocks out from under the tire that was stuck and then angled a mat under it. Mark got behind the wheel. A minute later, the shovels and mats were stored. We all climbed back into the truck and drove on toward Kalacha.

Later, a rock became wedged between two of our four back tires. Mark pulled over, knowing something was amiss from the tug of the steering wheel. Again, we all got out to watch. He studied the rock and then simply pried it out with a tire iron. A short, thin Kenyan man dressed in rags emerged from a mud hut to offer advice in Swahili to Mark, who did not speak Swahili. Mark, often annoyed when random strangers suddenly became experts on Mercedes trucks, glared at the man, who then turned to me.

"Muskrat? Muskrat?" He seemed to be saying.

"No, thank you," I said politely. "I don't need a muskrat."

Disappointed—perhaps by my lack of understanding or perhaps by the loss of his morning's entertainment—the little man stood watching as we drove away.

Our tires had been shredding along the edges from driving over the volcanic rocks since Loyangalani. The crew had studied the tires carefully. There were no jokes. There was only gloomy silence. They were obviously concerned. We had spare tires, but we did not have six spare tires.

PAZ lurched and struggled again. We had become stuck in gravel a second time. Again the crew quickly dug us out.

In midafternoon we reached a community camp in the small oasis town of Kalacha. The Kenyans here differed from the Kenyans we'd seen farther south. Many had lighter skin, and they wore multicolored scarves and flowing sarongs. They were beginning to bear a resemblance to Ethiopians. Area children would spot us and start running, chasing the truck at top speed until we outdistanced them, leaving them laughing by the side of the road.

Kalacha itself featured some concrete huts on a tiny dirt road. It was so remote that it wasn't even possible to replenish our diminishing supplies of soft drinks and beer. It did, however, have a windmill-powered source of water that made the hostile desert a little friendlier. The whole town had water, and our rest camp featured tin shacks with showers and a nice, round, aboveground swimming pool.

"It's a giant dog bowl!" I declared. "A giant dog is going to come and lick us all to death."

I was clearly suffering great boredom. At tremendous personal peril, nearly everyone went for a swim. Silence became laughter, and laughter turned to chatter as we rinsed away the sweat and dust of the day's drive.

Reenergized by the refreshing swim, we were helping Sam make pasta with canned meat chunks when Dragoman's locally based northern Kenya guide, Duva, walked up. He'd come from Marsabit to meet us. Many tourism companies employ local guides, not only because it is the most sensible way to get things accomplished on the road, but because it helps spread tourism dollars to the locals and makes it easier for tourists and locals to get to know each other a little bit.

Leaving Mark and Duva to discuss the next day's drive, I turned in early to the sanctuary of my little blue tent, its nylon walls my only semblance of privacy. Kalacha was small, and while there may have been something to do if I'd looked hard enough, I was tired from the drive-induced boredom of the day. And it was windy and dusty. I'd be glad to leave in the morning.

Before leaving Kalacha's giant dog bowl at seven the next morning, Mark first conferred quietly with Duva and the codriver, and then he briefed us on the day's agenda.

"We need to reach Marsabit by early afternoon to line up a guard for tomorrow."

We all looked at him inquisitively.

"From Marsabit to the Ethiopian border, we need an armed guard. It's a dangerous area. Sometimes trucks get shot at. The violence is generally not directed at tourists, but we are required to take a guard along. It's a deterrent."

Of course.

"There are two routes to Marsabit from here. The way we usually go takes us over more volcanic rock. Right now, this is a bad idea because our tires are already deteriorating from yesterday's drive from Loyangalani. The alternative is to go over the salt pans. In the wet season, this route is impassable, but it hasn't rained in months. We should be okay."

We took down our tents, washed and flapped the breakfast dishes, and boarded PAZ. Duva sat where he could talk to Mark, in the first row of seats. His sister, who had business in Marsabit, sat beside him with her baby in her lap.

We passengers had high hopes for Marsabit.

"I hope there's a launderette," said Monica. "The guidebook only lists a dry cleaner."

I was hoping for an Internet café. The last one had been a week ago in Isiolo.

Marsabit, according to my guidebook, didn't have a lot to offer. Still, it had a few hotels and supermarkets and was the last "real" town in northern Kenya.

We headed out into the desert again, across the dry salt pan. In a few hours, we'd have cold drinks and chocolate.

File under seemed-like-good-idea-at-the-time, I thought later. Sure, the dry, crusty salt pan hadn't had rain in months. But salt pans save their water for a nonrainy day by secreting it under the surface in a thick, damp layer of clay.

Sam was bored early in the day, so he wandered back for a chat, as he often did. I asked him about the Dragoman manual's instructions for driving in sand. He was hoping to learn to drive trucks, and he'd been slowly memorizing the entire manual. I suggested to him that my friend Nikki's system for driving in sand was best—she would slalom the front wheels to clear a path for the rear tires to grip the ground—but he argued that it was hard on the steering box. Nikki had driven for Dragoman for years and once shepherded me across India and the Middle East on Oscar, the truck I'd seen in Nairobi.

Suddenly, the truck lurched dramatically to the left, throwing us all about like basketballs. We thudded to a firm, definite halt. Mark tried gunning the gas and then put the truck into reverse. He rocked

PAZ forward and backward, but we couldn't move anywhere. We were tilted precariously to the left at a 25-degree angle.

Our crew got out and had a look.

"Fuck," said the normally unflappable Mark, at which point we realized we were in serious deep doo-doo as such unprofessional comments never escaped his lips in front of us.

We all got out to have a look. It turned out not to be doo-doo at all, but a trench of gray, dense clay.

"A case of classic salt-pan syndrome," explained Mark later.

Overland-truck legend has it that a Dragoman truck was once stuck in a Bolivian salt pan for nine days. Another road tale suggested that a competing company once had to abandon a truck altogether after attempting to mat out using the truck's own seats.

Later, when just the two of us were chatting, Mark would tell me that a few minutes before we crashed through the crusty surface, Duva had casually mentioned that another overland truck had gotten stuck in the same spot a few weeks earlier. Mark had glanced at Duva and kept his mouth shut. There was no point in yelling at him: "Why didn't you tell me this before I opted out of the volcanic rock route?"

But for now, Mark couldn't get angry as he had a situation to deal with.

"I'm not inclined to rush into this," he said. "We're not getting out of here any time soon. Shall we have tea?"

Sam pulled out a gas burner and put a kettle on to boil. Mark and Tony, both old hands at this sort of thing, discussed our options. Sam was also experienced in bogs—he'd been in Malawi as Nikki's cook during her six-day bog in '99. The road had collapsed under Nikki's truck during a downpour. Another truck had come to pull her truck out and had also gotten stuck. The passengers all had to camp in the rain alongside the truck for days, while they rebuilt the road with the help of local people who were employed on the spot. Every night, the rain would wash away some of the progress they'd made during the day.

We all drank tea and contemplated our sunken vehicle. It didn't move. *Was our extremely competent staff going to get us out of this bog? What if they couldn't?* Nobody said a word.

Finally, Mark, Tony, Sam, and Duva took shovels and disappeared under the truck. Charles enthusiastically went with them. Bits of clay started to fly out. The rest of us tried to help but it was pointless. One passenger tried to make progress with a tiny garden shovel and gave up in disgust, saying, "I might as well be using an emery board." I happily volunteered for nonfilthy beverage duty and made tea for those with clay-caked fingers.

Preliminary digging completed, we unlocked the sand mats. They were shoved under the tires. Mark started up the truck and accelerated.

PAZ sunk deeper. Mark cut the engine off.

Duva offered to walk back to Kalacha to find a tractor to haul us out. It would be a two-hour hike, but there were few options. He took a flask of water and set off, while I tried to amuse his sister's baby with a tennis ball. The baby seemed perfectly happy to be sitting in the middle of the desert. Everyone else was becoming restless.

Some discussed the possibility of making clay pots with our free time. Mark flew his power kite. It dipped and roared through the sky.

After an hour or so of lazily sitting in the midday sun and worrying about getting burned, I wandered off to a fringe of palms at the edge of the desert to sit in the shade. I sat on a rock for a while and sang a song, evidence that I was indeed bored out of my skull. Maybe if I sat there long enough, the tractor would be there when I returned.

It wasn't, although a few skinny local men had materialized out of nowhere to observe and offer unsolicited advice.

"No matter where you are in Africa," Mark told me later on, "even in the most remote place imaginable with no one in sight, once you stop, people will materialize out of nowhere."

The group had tired of inactivity and cooked an early lunch. We had run out of fresh food a few days ago, so lunch was once again "pasta surprise" with a sauce made of canned meats and vegetables.

The wind kicked up, blowing fine reddish dirt across the desert. The real surprise in "pasta surprise" turned out to be its gritty texture, which we all consumed without complaint.

Three hours after Duva left us, we were still sitting—bored and sunburned—in the middle of the desert.

"How long does it take to get a tractor?" someone groused.

Three hours was enough. The crew decided to take action. Perhaps, they assumed, Duva had encountered a setback. What if there was only one tractor in Kalacha? What if it was broken? They had to explore other options.

Mark instructed us all to fetch rocks and wood to put under the tires, but I suspect he just wanted to keep us occupied and out of harm's way while the crew executed a dangerous jacking operation.

PAZ was equipped with several jacks. Normally, they'd be used to elevate the truck for repairs. Today, the jacks were going to be used to lift the truck. Mark and Tony positioned blocks of wood and spare tires under the truck at key points and then placed the jacks on top of these secure positions. They pumped the jacks up. The idea was to lift the truck and then put the debris in the clay trenches underneath, so that we would be raising the left side inch by inch. In reality, all we managed to do was drive the jacking blocks deep into the clay.

Finally, after hours of trial and error with the jacks, they managed to slightly raise the truck. The passengers tipped rocks and debris into the grooves under the sunken wheels.

Just then, five hours after he'd left, Duva appeared on the horizon. In a tractor.

"Now remember," Mark reminded us cheerfully. "We are glad to see Duva and not angry that he's been gone so long."

We were delighted to see him for at least a minute. Then the tractor crew latched a steel cable onto PAZ's rear and pulled. The truck ended up deeper in the clay, at a more alarming angle than it had been before our crew had started the jacking.

It was time for Plan B. Or C. Or D. I'd lost track.

The tractor crew went off to collect large stones to build a new road underneath PAZ's wheels. Tony and Mark went back to work on the jacks, helped by Charles and Sam. The rest of us abandoned our dignity and cowered in a pack under the lunch table, which provided the sole square of shade in the entire desert.

The tractor returned with the stones and promptly got bogged in clay itself. I felt a surge of panic—if the tractor got stuck, we'd be camping here tonight—but then the tractor driver used the bucket as a crutch to lift the tractor up and out of the ground.

The jacks went up, the rocks and sand mats went down, and finally, after Mark drank a bit more tea, the truck moved a few degrees closer to its natural state.

There was more digging, more jacks, and more rocks. I was still preoccupied with cowering, and in spite of hiding from the sun, several of us got sunburned noses that took weeks to vanish.

Finally, ten hours and a lot of mud and tea later, PAZ was pulled triumphantly out of the clay and back onto the salty desert crust. Mark later explained to me that the goal in a bog is to keep the truck above the "point of departure." A well-balanced Dragoman Mercedes has a much higher point of departure than an overloaded cargo truck, a point proven to me with gusto a month later in an Isuzu in Ethiopia.

We returned to Kalacha for more pasta surprise. We were a lot more appreciative of the showers and swimming pool this time. Kalacha seemed like a slice of paradise after our day of sitting in mud and sun. Tomorrow we'd collect Duva's sister and her baby and try again.

"A.W.A.," said Charles.

"What's that?" I asked.

"Africa Wins Again," he said, laughing.

Chapter 15

Youyouyou, Faranji!

In a repeat of yesterday morning, we collected Duva, his sister, and his sister's baby to head off to Marsabit. But this time we made it. We drove the volcanic rock route and arrived in Marsabit in time for lunch, our tires intact but shredded.

The "best" hotel in town didn't have room for our group. We ended up next door at Dikus Hotel, which turned out to be fine, with clean pit toilets and electric-heated showers at one end.

Monica and I went to hunt for chocolate and encountered a traffic jam of two bicycles and three goats. Marsabit had no launderette, to Monica's disappointment, and certainly had no Internet access. It was a rinky-dink town, although it was a thriving metropolis compared to everywhere we'd been in the last few days.

The supermarket didn't have chocolate and, in fact, didn't have much of anything.

"Don't waste your time," said Sam, who as truck cook had headed straight to the supermarket. "All it has is soap and cereal."

Of course we went anyway and discovered that while harsh, Sam's assessment hadn't been entirely off base. What if, we worried, there were *no* chocolate in Marsabit? Food—particularly treats—takes on inflated significance on the road. Then, after twenty minutes of diligently visiting each store, we found (with some relief) a tiny shack on the main street that sold Cadbury bars.

A ten-year-old kid standing beside me at the counter demanded, "Give me money."

"Why should I?" I asked him.

He laughed and moved on. He hadn't really wanted money after all. It had been some kind of a test, or maybe a joke.

Monica and I walked on aimlessly, happily munching our stale chocolate—the first we'd seen since Nairobi. A group of children spotted us and took off running toward us at breakneck speed.

"No," we called over. "We're *eating* our candy. This candy is for us." We'd earned it.

Giggling, the kids stopped and left us alone.

Standing outside a wooden hut with soft drinks for sale, we admired an attractive goat.

"You can take its photo," offered a shoe-repair man who was standing next door outside his shop.

"I don't want to have to pay it," I joked.

Indignantly, he explained to me that there are many poor people in Kenya, but that I surely would not have to pay the goat for its photo.

Embarrassed, humbled, and mortified that I'd allowed such an insulting joke to escape my lips, I talked with the shoe-repair guy for a while. We chatted about the weather and about my shoes, which were dusty but not in need of repair. I also felt obliged to shoot a photo of the goat.

He was a nice fellow who was just looking to converse and pass some time. It was a switch from chatting with other Dragoman passengers over plates of Sam's food.

Monica and I drank a Coke each with our new friend, and then we moved on.

"I wonder where I can buy a newspaper," I mused to Monica.

Two boys overheard me and proceeded to escort us from store to store until we tracked down a copy of the weekly *East African* newspaper.

Monica and I were thrilled with Marsabit. It was a crummy little town in many ways, but we found its citizens to be charming.

Rain poured hard on the morning we left East Africa, encouraging us to pack quickly for our drive to the border town of Moyale. We collected an armed guard for the morning's drive, as bandits frequently shoot at trucks along the Moyale road. Shootings were directed more at commercial vehicles than at tourists, but having a man on board carrying a large semiautomatic weapon was a good insurance policy. He stood in the front, looking quite effective in his job as deterrent. No one shot at us. We were lucky—famed travel writer Paul Theroux's transport had been shot at earlier in the same year.

The drive was short—we rattled our way to the border over dirt roads in just a few hours with no mishaps—but clearing immigration took three hours. The Kenyan side was easy, but getting into Ethiopia involved three queues for each passenger. First, we had to get our passports stamped. Second, we had to show our yellow fever vaccine certificates. Finally, Customs looked at our bags (and in a few cases, actually opened them) and then took our currency declarations. And once the passengers had all made it through to the Ethiopia side, the truck had to go through border formalities. We sat bored, waiting, until 5:30 PM, when we finally cruised into Moyale, Ethiopia, to marvel at the smooth, paved road.

"Youyouyou!" screamed the Ethiopian children when they saw us.

Unfortunately, there was no room at the inn in Moyale. Some sort of conference was in town, and all the rooms were booked. We went minutes up the road to Bekele Molla Hotel, which was also fully booked, but it had a few rooms that were in the process of being renovated. We could stay in those rooms if we didn't mind "roughing it."

They weren't horrible. Or actually, some of them weren't. Monica and I scored a room with running water, no bathroom door, and a lot of mosquitoes.

But the door locked and the sheets were clean. I erected my mosquito net over my bed. Monica and I agreed to alert the other when either of us was in the bathroom.

Some of the others didn't fare so well. Tony's room was so bad that he asked reception to clean it. Reception sent down a crew, but the crew just looked, laughed, and walked away. He slept in his swag— a mini-tent with a built-in mattress and sleeping bag—instead.

After a dinner of beef curry around the truck, Mark lectured us on Ethiopia.

"When you hear the children scream 'youyouyou' at you, it means nothing. They are just excited to see you, and it is the English equivalent of something not impolite in Amharic. So expect to hear it a lot, and don't be offended by it.

"The same goes for the word *faranji*. It means 'foreigner,' and they use it to describe you. It is not meant as an insult.

"Ethiopia is a tough country to travel in, but it is also a rewarding country. Some say that it is the India of Africa, so for those of you who have been to India, that may mean something."

That meant something to me. I had found India difficult when I'd been there in '98. I'd been unaccustomed to the crowds and the poverty, and I had not known how to react to the constant begging I'd encountered in some areas.

"Also, Ethiopians are modest and conservative in dress. No short shorts. Everyone must cover their shoulders at all times. Ladies, no tank tops, and the bras have to go back on. Sorry.

"This next rule is somewhat embarrassing to mention, but it is a *major* rule here and you *must* obey it."

Mark paused, clearly relishing the moment. He took a deep breath.

"No farting," he said.

The passengers laughed. Most of us were relieved—our truck

had become too stinky lately, and the smelly noises were clearly coming from one or two sources.

"Now I know at home some of you may fart in front of your friends and you all have a good laugh over it, but it simply isn't done here."

I later read in my Lonely Planet *Ethiopia, Eritrea, and Djibouti* guidebook that Ethiopians find public flatulence barbaric, and that they consider the Italians and the French the worst offenders. They claim that the French are masters of the "silent but deadly" gas.

Our evening introduction to Ethiopia consisted only of Mark's lecture, a drink at the hotel bar, and more of Sam's cooking. The next morning, we were introduced to Ethiopian bureaucracy at the town bank. It took an hour and a half to change money. The amount of paperwork required for thirteen people to change traveler's checks was mind-boggling. Different officials, it seemed, were required to sign multiple copies of documents. We faced additional formalities— the security guard confiscated everyone's cigarettes, lighters, and pocketknives while we were inside.

As we drove north out of Moyale, I realized I'd been harboring a grudge against Ethiopia.

My mother had had an Eritrean foster daughter for a while. Sophie and her sister had escaped the war, traveling on camels across the desert to Sudan, where they'd been arrested for wearing "indecent" shorts that their uncle had sent them from the States. The Eritrean–Ethiopian War is a sensitive, emotional subject for Eritreans, and I'd been unconsciously sympathetic to Eritrea at the expense of Ethiopia. As we drove along the perfectly paved two-lane road watching impoverished Ethiopians carrying plastic jugs of water on donkeys, I realized that the average Ethiopian had as much to do with the war as I did with a typical U.S. military operation. That is, nothing.

The countryside had turned to lush, green hills with a single band of black asphalt cutting through and into the hills. Southwest Ethiopia—a few hours' drive to our left—was undergoing a famine, and this seemed unbelievable given our fertile surroundings.

Ethiopia's food-distribution system—stretched thin during times of regional famine—leaves some areas without, while other areas have too much food.

Occasionally, small drab towns would pop up alongside the road, their concrete single-room buildings open in front. People lined the roads—standing or walking—along with goats, donkeys, horses, and dogs. All people, animals, and vehicles equally used the road for transportation. Children chased our truck and screamed "youyouyou *faranji*" at the tops of their lungs. Every single one of them waved enthusiastically. We always waved back, and I wondered briefly if it were possible to get carpal tunnel syndrome from repetitive waving.

I had not enjoyed being on the truck in Kenya. It had been dull, suffocating, and claustrophobic. But with the overwhelming possibilities of Ethiopian culture being full-on and in my face, I suddenly was pleased to have an experienced and appreciative guide. I was glad for the refuge of the truck and even of the group. When the going got tough, I could rest in the tourist bubble. I wouldn't burn out on the challenges of Ethiopia. The truck trip would minimize the difficulties, allowing me to appreciate the country's positive aspects.

Mark was pleased to discover that a smooth, new road had been built at the turnoff for our hotel. He was not so pleased ten minutes later when he discovered that the hotel had been demolished to make room for the road.

"I don't know where there's another hotel," he told us. "We might have to drive another three hours to Dila." It was already dark, and Ethiopia—with its high-traffic roads full of goats and dogs and people—was not a good place to drive in the dark.

Luck was with us. A few miles down the road, we stumbled onto a good hotel with a parking lot and secure, clean rooms. We all got our own.

"In Ethiopia, you will find that most rooms are either singles or have double beds. There are very few twin rooms, and the idea of backpackers traveling together is fairly new here," said Mark. "So if you would all start hooking up, it would save us money."

He was joking, but we all eyed each other warily. No one felt any sparks whatsoever on this leg of the trip.

We cooked sausage and potatoes in the parking lot and then stopped in the hotel bar for a nightcap. With faded couches and '70s paneling, it looked like someone's parents' basement rec room. A few enthusiastic men were there, dancing alone, and a woman in a sleeveless evening gown stood at the bar. It was all rather depressing, so I went to sleep, reveling in my own room.

In the morning, our nice hotel in the middle of nowhere had no power or light. And the water had been turned off too. It helped us get ready quickly, as we threw on clothing by candlelight.

We reached Shashamene, the transport capital of southern Ethiopia, in midmorning. Mark warned the group to be careful—

Shashamene had a xenophobic edge to it, and the last time he'd been here children had thrown rocks at the truck.

Instead of the steady refrain "youyouyou," I heard "fuckfuckfuck" at least once, and it was clearly aimed in our direction. Mark devised a plan to keep the truck moving so it wouldn't be a target.

First, he dropped off the rest of the passengers at a café and told them to stay put. Then he took Sam and a few shopping helpers to the outdoor food market and left them there to stock up on supplies. Finally, he took me to the bus station so that I could catch a bus to Addis Ababa.

I was leaving the group for a few days. They were going to camp in the Bale Mountains National Park. I was opting out of this excursion because I needed to get to work on acquiring a visa for Sudan. This could be tricky under the best of circumstances, as Sudan was a country at war, and it wasn't clear how (if at all) the events of September 11 might affect officialdom's perceptions of a lone American's backpacking through the northern part of the country.

I also needed some time alone and some breathing room. I recently had learned to appreciate the bubble of Westerners inside the truck, but I would still be happy to have a few days of space.

Mark parked the truck inside the bus station lot, which meant we were less likely to have rocks thrown at us. I left him, agreeing that we'd meet in Addis Ababa at Bel-Air Hotel later in the week. I walked toward the buses, calling out "Addis Addis" as I went. Friendly men pointed me in the right direction, toward a long, crowded bus. Buses run daily along the Moyale–Addis Ababa route, with a stopover in Shashamene.

I bought one of the last two "seats." In Ethiopia, the rule is that everyone must have a seat. Standing in the aisle is forbidden. Once the real seats are gone, little wooden stools take over. As a guest, I was not subjected to the little wooden stool. The conductor cleared a seat for me on a metal box just behind the driver. My feet hung over the side, and my right side faced the bus.

The entire bus had an excellent view of the metal box, perfect for watching the strange activities of one blond *faranji*. As I bought my ticket, an old woman with cataracts butted her head into my hip repeatedly until I gave her some coins.

Distorted Ethiopian music blared from the bus speakers. I shifted my butt on the hard metal case and we roared out of the bus park and the rock-throwing town of Shashamene.

With guilty relief, I spotted the Dragoman truck driving off into the distance—without me. I was a solo traveler again.

Fifty Ethiopians and I turned the opposite direction, onto the road to Addis. Perched on the metal box behind the driver, I had an excellent vantage point for viewing green Lake Langano, a popular Ethiopian Rift Valley resort area. We sped through small towns brimming with chickens, goats, horse-drawn carts, and bicycles.

Every time I looked back down the aisle of the bus, fifty people smiled and tried to get my attention. Friendly, challenging Ethiopia. I was going to like it here.

A toddler, Francis, sat behind me with his parents. I introduced him to the zipper-puller I had on my pack, a mangy stuffed Tasmanian devil. He tugged on it. Fifty passengers giggled. I pulled Taz's string, making him appear to move of his own accord. The kid looked confused, and the passengers howled with laughter.

Later, Francis's mom, laden with baby gear, accidentally bumped me first in the butt and then in the head. The bus passengers went into hysterics.

I had never felt so hilarious and had never had an audience that was so easily pleased.

The mom played patty-cake with Francis and then sang him the months of the year, both in English and in Amharic. The kid sang along, pausing uncertainly at "December." He clapped, and they started again.

The bus passed a dead man lying sprawled by the side of the road. He was naked from the waist down. The Ethiopians all looked at each other with concern, and at me with some embarrassment, but the bus roared on. I was startled, then disturbed, but I shrugged. *What could have happened to that man?* I would never know.

I thought back to the guidebook's warning about Ethiopian buses and wished it had been wrong. As the book had pointed out, Ethiopians refuse to open windows on buses. They think it will make them sick. So I was encountering this bit of irrationality firsthand, and it was damned hot.

But the good news? In Ethiopia, no one farts in public.

Chapter 16

Addled in Addis

I awoke early to a sun-drenched room. Africa had changed my sleeping habits. In my previous life as a freelancer, I'd worked well into every night and never awoken before nine. But days began with sunrise in Africa, and if I wanted to go anywhere or get anything done, I had to adhere to the local schedule.

Breakfast was included with the price of my room at Buffet de la Gare. I had come to expect a fried egg and greasy meat as my free breakfast in most places, so I was pleased to get fresh-squeezed orange juice, three slices of thick toast, and delicious Ethiopian espresso.

Ethiopia has a credible claim to being the birthplace of coffee, and it proudly produces rich, dark beans for local consumption as well as export. As a coffee snob, I had been on a lucky streak. Every country I'd visited in East Africa—Tanzania, Uganda, Kenya, and Ethiopia—had produced excellent, unique, fresh java.

The actual "buffet" part of Buffet de la Gare was a hot nightspot, and the thumping bass of the band had gone on very late. The stale smell of tobacco was no doubt permanent in the restaurant and competed with the coffee aroma.

After a quick shower, I wrestled with the toilet until realizing that I had to open up the back and fill the tank manually. But I didn't mind. Every budget traveler is a skilled toilet technician, and I was excited to be on my own in Ethiopia.

I'd raced to Addis to begin paperwork on my Sudanese visa. My ongoing transportation—the ferry to Europe, the ship home from England—was a house of cards that rested on getting this sticker in my passport. But it was Sunday. The Sudanese embassy was closed. Banks were closed too, so I took a 15 birr taxi to the Hilton to change money. A farmer was herding his goats down the street in front of the Hilton, toward the UN African headquarters.

The sights were open, so after changing money, I went to the National Museum to see "Lucy," the oldest nearly complete human remains found to date. Actually, the real remains are stored in a vault. The tiny skeleton on display is a modern duplicate.

Then it was off to see Abyssinian lions, the rare black-maned Ethiopian lions. I got to the zoo just at feeding time, and I watched with interest as children were invited close to the cub cages for personalized photos. The kids would giggle, looking both thrilled and terrified.

The larger lions paced back and forth in their small concrete cells, waiting for their lunch, until the keeper threw a hunk of raw meat at each of them.

They all tore viciously into their hunks, as if they hadn't eaten for weeks.

A dilapidated taxi took me to the hip Piazza part of town, which was crowded with stores but still shabby. Everything there was closed on Sunday, except for Tomoco Coffee. I bought a kilo of Ethiopia's finest to drink later, when I'd rejoined the overland truck. Another customer helped me pick out some beans. By now it was lunchtime, so I asked him if there was a good restaurant nearby.

When will I learn? I thought later. Mention what you need and not only will people help you, they will hospitably insist on showing you the way, at which point you are socially obligated to break bread with them.

The man escorted me to the café.

"Do you mind if I sit down, too?" I knew full well the protocol. In Ethiopia, the host pays for lunch, and I was the host here. Chafing inwardly because I'd wanted only to quickly grab a bite and move on, I graciously indicated he could join me. I reminded myself that I was here for cultural experiences, that I should be more interested in other people while on the road.

"What is your job at home?" asked the man.

"Artist," I said. His eyes opened in apparent astonishment.

"I am also an artist," he declared.

That surprised me, though it wouldn't have farther south. In Tanzania and Zimbabwe, lots of people are artists. They make commercial art for tourists—sturdy bookends shaped like elephants, four-foot carved wooden giraffes, and soapstone ashtrays. But here in

Ethiopia, where tourism was not even yet in its infancy, I wondered if perhaps my new friend worked in the fine arts. Maybe he was a painter.

He pulled out a photo of one of his designs. To my disappointment, it looked like a factory-produced batik, not unlike hundreds I had seen farther south.

My lunch guest was too eager, in the end, as he desperately tried to convince me to come to his gallery. Not only did he give me directions ("on the Burger Queen Road between Shell and Mobil") and tell me when the gallery was open, he wanted to pick me up and escort me. Uncomfortable with his eagerness as such eagerness usually accompanies a hard sell, I made excuses.

After paying the bill for both our meals, I escaped into a taxi, taking it only a few blocks before telling the driver I'd forgotten something and instructing him to pull over.

Alone again, I wandered down Churchill Avenue, where the shops are open every day, past the coffin shops—coffins are big business in much of Africa—and stopped in a souvenir store. A British woman sat in the dark, examining an antique metal crucifix by candlelight.

"Oh," I said. "Has the power gone out?"

"You haven't been in Addis very long, have you?" She laughed.

I shopped by flashlight, as it dawned on me that Ethiopia had amazing religious art. On display were intricate miniature carved wooden doors on hinges that opened to reveal colorful biblical paintings below, as well as silver seals, crucifixes, and sequential painted stories on canvas.

I bought a few trinkets—a steel Ethiopian cross and a wooden carving with a small door that opened to reveal Saint George and the Virgin Mary on opposing panels—before strolling back down Churchill Avenue. A jittery Ethiopian teenager took up step beside me and started speaking French.

"*Je ne parle pas de Français*," I said.

"I know," he replied, confusing me completely, before he started talking about his favorite movies.

He was a nice kid, and his imitations of all his favorite movie stars charmed me. He showed me how Wolverine's claws shot out in the *X-Men* movie, though I didn't bother trying to explain to him that I was not only acquainted with Wolverine from my past life as an X-Men comic-book colorist, but I knew decidedly geeky details about all his friends, enemies, adamantium skeleton, and past creators as well.

The teen escorted me to shops and introduced me to anyone who would pay attention.

I was starting to think that maybe the kid was just nice and not a smooth operator, when he doubled over in apparent but not very authentic-looking pain.

Yeah, right . . . I thought, but I said in an equally inauthentic tone of concern, "Are you okay?"

"I am just feeling very sick, because I have not eaten in a long time," he explained.

It was an awkward situation. The kid was obviously homeless—perhaps a glue-sniffer—and he needed food. I didn't think he should be pretending to be so sick in front of me, but I didn't think I'd have just given him money if he'd asked for it right out. I felt bad and ethically challenged, as I often was when someone asked me for money. I gave him some birr, even as I wondered if he would really eat with it or if he were abusing glue as so many children of the streets do. He thanked me and walked away.

Ethiopia is one of the world's poorest countries and many people there are destitute. Mark had told us, in his lecture on Ethiopia, that we should not be afraid to give to beggars.

"You won't be ruining it for other tourists. Even the local people give to beggars, so just follow their example and give a few coins here and there. Don't give a lot, or tourists will become a target. And you can't give to everyone, so try to pick a cause."

I had chosen crippled women and destitute children, but I rapidly found myself giving to anyone who was disabled.

Later, I left my hotel to find dinner and passed a couple with their little girl walking outside the train station.

The little girl was around six years old, and she was dressed in a frilly pink satin dress. Her parents each held one of her hands, but when she saw me, she slowly, deliberately removed her right hand from her mother's. She stuck it out to me, smiling. I shook it and her eyes lit up.

Her parents beamed their approval. My faith in total strangers in Ethiopia was restored. Not everyone was looking for a handout.

The next morning, it was time to enact Plan A—forge ahead through Sudan.

Plan B, in case I didn't manage to get a Sudanese visa, was to take the train to Djibouti and catch a ship from there.

But there was no apparent train schedule, and the only railway employee I could find gave me just a vague approximation of when the train might leave. He shoved me away as the train from the coast arrived and the masses disembarked, so I caught a taxi to the Embassy of Sudan.

I tapped on the metal gate in the wall at the Sudanese embassy. A guard poked his head out and let me in.

"Sign in," he said, pointing to a book. He took my passport.

"USA. Great!" he exclaimed. I felt a little bravado, but I was mostly scared that I'd be turned down flat. I'd heard the Sudanese Embassy required letters of recommendation from the applicant's home embassy. I'd also heard that the U.S. Embassy did not issue recommendations.

"Where's the visa section?" I asked the guard.

"See that pickup truck? Go in the door next to it."

I walked, jittery and shaking a little, across the parking lot to enter a dark room.

A tall Sudanese man with frizzy white hair said, "Why do you want to go to Sudan?"

"Transit to Egypt," I responded.

Bzzzt . . . wrong answer. He looked at me disapprovingly.

"Why not just fly to Cairo?"

I explained my mission.

"I am traveling without planes. I want to go through Sudan. But maybe this is a problem," I said, sliding my passport across the desk to him.

He looked furious.

"You hate us," he said.

"I personally don't hate anyone . . ." I started, but he cut me off.

"I know, I know. I don't mean the people. I mean America."

I changed the subject.

"I want to see the pyramids at Meroe. Do you know them?"

"Look behind you."

The pyramids of Sudan adorned a calendar on the wall.

"Yes, yes! Those pyramids." I had never seen a photo of them before.

"Why don't you apply for a tourist visa?" he suggested, suddenly kinder. I crossed out "transit" on my application and wrote in "tourist."

"Two photos and $60."

I forked it over, while he muttered that America hates Muslims.

"I personally . . ." I began.

"I know, I know," he grumbled. "They think we are all terrorists."

"That's why I want to go, to show it's safe." *Had I found an angle?*

He smiled warmly, gave me a claim check, and told me to telephone on Wednesday at noon. I had been warned earlier by email to follow his instructions precisely by Australian writer Peter Moore, who had had to work a lot harder at his visa application than I had to. Perhaps I'd get to see the pyramids at Meroe after all.

When I left to walk back to the Buffet de la Gare, I passed another dead man, sprawled with both arms stretched out. The one I'd seen from the bus had been missing his pants, but this man's shirt was missing and his ankles were bound. A policeman had just arrived on the scene and was getting off his motorbike with a pad of paper. I hurried by.

The dead guy and policeman were both gone the next time I passed.

It was a bad morning.

I was starting to crack. Fascinating Ethiopia, with its anonymous dead men, limbless beggars, and glue-sniffing street children, was taking its toll on me. I was tired of seeing maimed people crawling on all fours, flip-flops on their hands as well as on their feet. I was frustrated with the pace of progress on my own work. When I'd spent Tuesday coding for my website, the Internet was so slow that I felt as if I could've just typed in zeros and ones instead of hitting enter.

And I was nervous. Today was the day that would determine my immediate future. If I got a Sudanese visa, I'd be set. If not, I'd have to take a train to Djibouti and hope my cargo-ship agent could find me a ship. *Was that even possible? How long would it take?* There was no way to know. And it was the wrong time of the month.

Nevertheless, in the face of escalating inconvenience, I didn't crack instantly. But before too long, I fell to pieces in the face of things that didn't seem to be a big deal at all.

I had a bag of things to send home, including the religious souvenirs I'd bought in Ethiopia, my point-and-shoot camera that I'd broken last week when I'd smacked it against the side of the truck, a large wooden hippo I'd bought in Nairobi, and a marble egg with a map of the world painted on it. I packed it all carefully, using the last of my tape and bubble wrap. I got up early and went to the post office.

The security guards—there are security guards at all Ethiopian government offices and most respectable businesses as well—inspected my bag. They were just about to let me in when one of them held up my Canon, barely visible through its protective bubble wrap.

"Camera," the guard announced, confiscating it and giving me a claim check.

"No," I said, grabbing it back. "I'm posting that."

The guards stared at me. They spoke no English aside from "camera," and they didn't know what I was talking about.

I mimed a flying plane with my hand and put my camera on it. "United States," I said. "Canon, warranty."

They still wouldn't let me go. I was astonished and starting to slowly boil. The camera was broken, unreachable in its bubble wrap, and why on earth wouldn't they let me in the post office with a camera anyway? Were they afraid I'd photograph their stamp collections?

Annoyed, I stalked off. A few minutes later, I encountered more frustration at the other entrance.

"But the camera is broken," I said. I put it on the ground and motioned stomping on it. "I must send to America."

The guard grasped my plan and understood my problem. He took the camera, in its bubble wrap, and escorted me to the parcel counter. He showed the camera to the clerk and explained what I wanted.

"*No*," said the clerk, pushing the camera aside.

The guard tried again and was sternly spoken to. He apologized and left with the camera. I could retrieve it at the gate.

The situation seemed ludicrous. I was going to have to carry a broken camera to Egypt because of the strange rules of the Ethiopian postal system.

I handed over the rest of my parcel. The clerk went through and pulled out my souvenirs.

"Permit," he said. "You must get permit."

I knew permits were required to export antiques from Ethiopia, but my souvenirs were all brand-new, designed to look antiquelike. They were obviously not state treasures.

"These are new," I argued. "They cost just a few dollars. Do you think I could get an antique for $2?"

He didn't care. He was erring on the extreme side of caution.

"Fine. Where do I get a permit?" I asked in an exasperated tone.

"Department of Antiquities."

"Where's that?" I expected it to be the next counter, or perhaps upstairs.

"National Museum," he said. I stared at him in disbelief. That was on the other end of town. Was I really required to taxi across town, go through an in-triplicate paperwork process of certifying that my new souvenirs were not antique, then taxi back, check my camera, and wait in line again?

Apparently, yes. He dismissed me.

I could feel tears of frustration welling, but I subdued them. I marched down the street to DHL, where the clerk told me I could mail all but the hippo for $100.

$100! That was an excessive price to pay for the paranoia of the Ethiopian postal system. And I couldn't carry this massive hippo through Sudan, where I'd be hitching rides on the backs of trucks.

Now thoroughly depressed, I caught a taxi to the National Museum. I knew the going rate was 10 birr within town, and 15 birr for tourists, but I was preoccupied with my mailing problem so I didn't state the fare clearly before I got in.

The driver took the longest possible route and then declared "30 birr" when we pulled up at the National Museum.

This was the last straw for me. The taxi driver and I had a shouting match that ended with my throwing the 30 birr at him. Later, I'd hit upon (and use) the idea of not negotiating. I'd get out first and then hand back the correct fare through the window. I could then walk off no matter what the driver yelled after me.

Teary-eyed, I took my wooden hippo and souvenirs into the Department of Antiquities.

"What is the matter, madam?" said the young man who worked there.

"Fight with taxi driver," I said, not thinking it was appropriate to say, "Everything in Addis driving me bananas."

He surveyed my souvenirs and told me to take them all out of their bubble wrap, even though you could see everything clearly through the bubble wrap. He started to tear into them.

"No," I shrieked in horror. I carefully peeled off the bubble wrap that I'd bought in Nairobi. "I need that to post with."

He examined every item and filled out a form for each one. He got to the hippo.

"What is this?" he asked.

"Hippo," I said, though I supposed he could see that.

"Unwrap it." I did, and its back leg splintered into pieces and collapsed. The wooden hippo had seen better days.

"Where did you get this?"

"Kenya."

"I cannot give you a permit for something you got in Kenya," he declared.

"I can't mail it without a permit, but I can't get a permit?" I asked in disbelief.

"Right," he said, a bit sheepishly. He wouldn't give me a permit for a few other things that were obviously Kenyan—so I'd have to carry those across Sudan or throw them away—but when he got to my smaller wooden hippos, I just claimed they were Ethiopian.

The forms were stamped by an official—in triplicate—who apologetically said, "It is not our rule. I am sorry."

The young man took it upon himself to assist me. He told a taxi driver to take me back to the post office for 15 birr, and then he jumped in the front seat.

"I will help you," he declared.

"No, I can do it alone," I said. "Honest."

"No, I help," he repeated. And that was the end of it.

We went to the post office, where the clerk informed me that the mailing of my parcel—sea mail, minus the hippo, camera, and Kenyan souvenirs—would cost $40.

"It is foreigner-price," explained my helper.

"No. I cannot pay that."

Exasperated, I took my permits and souvenirs and left. My helper asked for a tip of 10 birr. Disgusted with the entire day, I forked it over.

I couldn't wait for the cocoonlike Dragoman truck to show up, to insulate me and rescue me from frustration. Gone were the days of annoyance at group fun.

And the days of group fun were almost here. But first, there was the small matter of my Sudanese visa. It was noon on Wednesday. I called the embassy.

"Your visa is ready," said an official. "Come by now."

I rushed to the Embassy of Sudan.

Wordlessly, a well-dressed man pushed my passport across a desk at me. The visa was there, and on page 35: Valid for one month.

"Thank you," I said, delighted. The frizzy white-haired man walked in and I thanked him too. I scampered out, eager to get back to my taxi before they changed their minds.

My earlier tears and frustration had turned to elation. Triumphantly, I caught a taxi to the Bel-Air. The Dragoman truck would be there by now. I marched into the lobby and sat down across from Mark, who was nursing a beer.

"I got it!" I said, shoving my passport in front of him. Mark was as surprised as I was that I had succeeded. My frustration at the Ethiopian postal system had evaporated. Addis Ababa was fascinating, and Ethiopia was a wonderful place.

To celebrate my good fortune, I threw away the broken hippo, and then I went over to DHL and paid $100 to ship the rest of my package home.

Chapter 17

Denial Ain't Just a River in Egypt, It's in Ethiopia, Too

The huge Dragoman Mercedes truck drove us past beggars, commuters, and joggers on its way out of Addis Ababa. Jogging is a national pastime in Ethiopia, and the country has a tradition of holding its own races in addition to sending champions to marathons throughout the world. After encountering so many unusual aspects of African bush and urban living during the last several months, I was startled to see runners casually getting their morning exercise. Morning jogging was so typical of my own world, left behind ten months ago.

At last, we were out in the countryside and on our way to the source of the Blue Nile, which meets the White Nile at Khartoum.

And I had learned my lesson about scoffing at the tourist bubble. I now valued my friends and was grateful for the presence of guides and a vehicle.

"Pen! Pen! Give me a pen!" Children waved frantically and chased our truck through town. We had just arrived in the small, dusty village of Dejen, an overnight stop en route to Lake Tana at Bahir Dar.

Our group was good at ignoring requests for pens by now and drove straight to a hotel. My little blue tent—so useful in Kenya—had gone into semiretirement, as there were few campgrounds in Ethiopia. Hotels were so cheap we stayed in them regularly.

Monica and I were sharing a room. We opened the shutters for a while, as the single lightbulb hanging from a ceiling cord emitted only faint light. But children hung in through the window and yelled with excitement.

"Youyouyou, *faranji!*"

We closed the window to unpack in dimness and silence.

While Sam cooked us dinner, someone called my attention to a small pet that lived inside the hotel restaurant.

"Marie, it's your friend."

Shyly peeking from behind the bar, with huge ears and a stripe down his nose, was a baby dik-dik.

I gasped and put my hand out toward my former adversary. The little dik-dik did not run away.

"May I touch it?" I asked the bartender.

"Pick it up," he suggested.

I gently scooped up the dik-dik. He was tiny and light but didn't flinch, nor did he try to eat me as I'd feared one would back in Kenya. I stroked his soft back, savoring the moment before placing him back on a bed of old blankets behind the bar.

The following afternoon took us along the perfectly paved main road to Bahir Dar, where we set up camp on the grounds of a hotel. Monica and I did our part for the local economy by getting a twin room for $13, complete with hot water and a veranda by Lake Tana.

If Ethiopia had tourist hot spots, the city of Bahir Dar would be one of them, along with Axum, Gonder, and Lalibela, the other sites on the "Historic Route." Not only is Bahir Dar the gateway to the Blue Nile Falls and the source of the Blue Nile, it features 15th-century island monasteries on Lake Tana.

In the next few days, our group took excursions first to the Blue Nile Falls, called Tisissat—meaning "water that smokes"—and then to Lake Tana monasteries and the source of the Blue Nile, or more accurately, the first big lake along the route of the source spring.

The source of the Ethiopian Nile has never been as publicly debated as has the source of the White Nile. Sure, a fair share of explorers have investigated the Ethiopian Highlands that are credited with originating the Ethiopian Nile branch, but it's never generated the publicity that the Uganda Nile has through the centuries. No doubt this is because a cast of luminaries—Speke, Burton, Livingstone, Baker, Stanley—sought the source of the White Nile during the great Victorian era of African exploration.

Our group traveled to the supposed source of the Nile by motorboat. Monica, seasick from the gently rolling waves and perhaps by a few beers she'd indulged in the night before, unceremoniously vomited into the source of the Nile, leaving her own rapidly diluting mark on the world's longest river.

Next, we chugged over to visit a few of the twenty or so Ethiopian Orthodox monasteries that dot the thirty-seven islands around Lake Tana.

Ethiopian Orthodox Christianity—sometimes confused with the Coptic Church because of past affiliations and similarities in origin—is full of fascinating, unique traditions. Many of its traditions seem straight out of the Old Testament, perhaps because the region was isolated for centuries, and the Ethiopian Orthodox bible includes books unknown to Protestants and Catholics. Some of these detail adventures in the lives of the Virgin Mary, King Solomon, and the Queen of Sheba.

Until recently introduced in Amharic, church communications traditionally were carried out only in the dead language of Ge'ez, similar to the way that the Vatican officially uses Latin. Ge'ez now is used only by priests and scholars.

The monasteries were round buildings with thatched roofs. Colorful paintings adorned the walls around the inner sanctums, telling stories from the Ethiopian Bible through the universal language of bright, appealing frescos and murals. To me, a comic-book colorist and editor, it looked like sequential storytelling.

We were not allowed access into the inner sanctums, as only the holiest can go there to approach each church's most valued possession— its *tabot*, or replica of a tablet from the Ark of the Covenant.

The real Ark, the powerful chest that purportedly holds the tablets inscribed with the Ten Commandments, was, according to

Ethiopians, brought south during the time of King Solomon, and after a long epic journey of hundreds of years, found its way to Axum and Saint Mary of Zion's Church, where it remains. Researchers have found nothing to support this claim, but they have found nothing to deny it either. Likewise, writer Graham Hancock, in his book *The Sign and the Seal*, concluded that it's certainly as likely as it is unlikely.

One of our scheduled monastery visits was to a men-only monastery.

Apparently a powerful Jewish warrior queen, Queen Judit, once razed the monasteries of Lake Tana, and no females have been allowed to the holiest places since then. Even female animals are kept away.

We women sniffed our disdain and visited a newer monastery, where a cross-eyed priest welcomed us and fed us some dry bread cooked by a local woman. We secretly knew we'd gotten the better end of the deal, but we tried not to rub it in when the guys returned.

Later, back at the hotel, a man in a pickup truck delivered us a new tire to replace one that had been worn out by the volcanic rock back in Kalacha. The pickup wouldn't start when it was time to leave. A group of men struggled to push-start the truck, but they seemed to need help so I joined them. They laughed at first, but I was strong from lugging my forty-pound backpack around the world for nearly a year. They didn't laugh a minute later when the truck started from our combined efforts.

"Need a ride?" asked the driver.

"Sure!" I called Monica over and we jumped into the back of the truck. I wanted to go to town and hunt for goatskin lunch boxes.

The lunch boxes were not really boxes but they were covered in goatskin. They were round like furry, overgrown coconuts with the tops lopped off. The tops were then put back into place and held there with goat-leather straps. *Injera* and spicy meat *tibs* or puréed vegetables were usually stored within. They were a specialty of the region, and despite having no need for a goatskin lunch box, I knew I had to have one.

A group of young men from the pickup truck–pushing incident accompanied us. They acted as our de facto guides, and they didn't seem to want anything from us. They were bored and just going along for an entertaining afternoon. Later, one asked me for a pen. I didn't have a spare.

I was not in Ethiopia to teach anyone a lesson. Surely, "You won't get a pen from attaching yourself to tourists" was a lesson well worth learning. *But what of the poverty, and what of my personal guilt? What was my responsibility? Was it to provide free creature comforts or to force some unrequested self-respect onto those who assumed the role of beggar?*

Once again, I was struggling with unanswerable questions. Westerners should not, I believed, encourage the perception that they are Santa Clauses by handing out little trinkets. It really aids only the ego of the giver. But one cannot ignore poverty or pretend that there's not a serious equity problem in the world, especially in light of the West's complicity in taking advantage of the resources and instability of places such as Ethiopia to pass on greater consumer advantages back home. I could get a pound of high-grade coffee beans in New York for less than $6, but African coffee farmers were starving.

I gave the young man some birr and thanked him for his assistance, again unhappy that I could not resolve my moral quandary.

The next morning's drive took us to the next hot spot on the Ethiopia tourist circuit. Gonder, with its 17th-century medieval castles, is often called the Ethiopian Camelot.

It is also the jumping-off point for public transit to Sudan, so I would be returning in just more than a week. I ran around and gathered information on transport and accommodation, and I checked my email to discover, to my great pleasure, that I could catch a *Grimaldi* freighter to Italy from Egypt or Israel in three weeks' time.

Satisfied that the last variable in Marie's World Tour was no longer in question, I toured the town and looked for a place to stay when I returned.

Two young men, Peter and Ababa, introduced themselves in the town center. They were part of the horde of Mark-idolizers, the dozens of Ethiopians who turned out to greet the Dragoman driver Mark every time he came to a major town. He seemed to be an icon in Ethiopian tourism. This extended to his passengers and meant that we were often elevated to a level of great respect simply by affiliation.

"What are you going to do today?" asked Peter.

"I don't know," I said. "Maybe check schedules at the bus station. Maybe I'll go to the pottery shop."

"You can go to the Falasha village to buy pottery there if you want."

I said sure, but I didn't want to pay a lot for a taxi. I was interested in Falasha Jews, after having read about how their Judaism, like

Ethiopian Christianity, had been undiluted by outside influences during centuries of isolation. Peter stayed behind with me for a minute while Ababa went to negotiate a horse-drawn carriage for us.

I had never seen such a thin, miserable horse, though I saw plenty more of them in the next ten days. We trotted up the road for a few miles, with Peter and Ababa eventually walking alongside the carriage once it became apparent that the horse was slower than most people.

The Falasha village seemed to have exactly one full-blooded Falasha Jew left, and she was reportedly looking for a sponsor to take her to Israel.

But the village had enough interest in Judaism to keep a mud hut-synagogue active and open.

"Shalom," I said to the last Falasha Jew in Gonder. She smiled appreciatively. I bought a piece of pottery from her, a black clamshell that opened to show the Queen of Sheba and King Solomon in bed together. According to the Kebra Negast book of the Ethiopian Bible, the Queen of Sheba was Ethiopian. She had traveled to Jerusalem, where she had conceived a son (Menelik) with King Solomon. Later, the son returned to Jerusalem to take the Ark of the Covenant home to Ethiopia.

On the buggy ride back to town, I asked Peter and Ababa why every kid I met in Ethiopia wanted pens. They told me the pens were for schoolwork.

"But what about if tourists give the pens to teachers, and they can distribute them, so that the kids don't have to beg the tourists?" I asked.

"Then the teachers keep the pens," replied Peter with finality.

They saw me back to the hotel and asked me to send a Bob Marley cassette when I could.

After another afternoon of touring the castles and churches of Gonder, we headed north toward Axum, stopping en route to set up camp in some foothills.

I erected my tent far away from the others, under a tree where I could listen to crickets and birds. In the morning, I awoke to unfamiliar voices chattering in low tones outside my tent. I took my time emerging. I knew that it would be local people, their curiosity bringing them out to stare at us, the freak show-on-wheels.

When I did emerge, eight pairs of eyes immediately swung over to rest on me. The owners of the eyes were all dressed in tatters, but that didn't mean anyone was here to beg. They were only watching. Later, when we offered our breakfast leftovers, the locals refused them until we pointed out that the beans on toast were vegetarian. It was, after all, one of Ethiopia's Orthodox Christian fasting days that come around twice a week.

I packed up my little blue tent with sorrow. I would not be using it again, and I was giving it to Monica for her continuing Dragoman trip, which would end in Nepal in February. It had provided me the illusion of privacy and control, and it had been a haven of sanity in an unrelenting group situation.

We continued our experience of floating through Ethiopia in a tourist bubble. It wasn't altogether unlike watching Ethiopia on TV, with the sound track blaring "youyouyou" all the time. Our drive took us through minuscule towns of mud huts and boys in donated

DARE T-shirts and rags. The smaller boys' heads were all shaved but for tufts of hair just above the foreheads. Our local Ethiopian guide said this was so that if they were to die, they could be lifted by God by their tuft-handle hair.

We arrived in the medium-size town of Axum just before lunch. Our local guide proudly told us that he had been the Axum guide mentioned in *The Sign and the Seal.* After he left, I presented Mark a paragraph in which the author had described the guide as spending "all his time in a brothel." Unfortunately, the guide had a prior engagement and was not able to guide us through the sights of Axum, and I could not ask him to autograph the paragraph in question.

We had a look at the archaeological museum and at the outside of the church that theoretically holds the Ark (though we weren't allowed inside), and then we walked to the nearby stelae field, accompanied by eager teenage boys trying to sell us Ethiopian crosses. One of them wore a T-shirt advertising a plumbing company on East 18th Street in Manhattan.

Stelae look an awful lot like obelisks. In fact, I am not altogether sure what the differences are between the two, even after later reading up on the subject. They are both granite pillars that end in a point, and they have carvings on the sides. Only 5 percent of the Axum stelae site has been excavated and archaeologists have hundreds of years of work ahead of them.

The tallest standing Axum stela—or obelisk—is seventy feet high, while the collapsed one directly across from Saint Mary's is 110 feet of fallen glory. Some believe that the power of the Ark was used to raise the stelae and to win "unwinnable" wars.

After an afternoon of touring sites, I took off alone into town to acquire an Ethiopian head scarf for my solo excursion into Sudan, and in every shop I went into, the shopkeeper tried to get me to take tea. I felt guilty fleeing, but I needed to get to the bus station to buy tickets. Monica and I were leaving the truck for the loop to Lalibela in the morning. I was leaving the truck for good, and I was both relieved and apprehensive about going back to solo travel. Monica would rejoin the Dragoman trip in five days to return to Addis and then fly to Cairo.

After dinner, I sat alone in the hotel room. Everyone else went to a disco, so when I came back outside later, only Mark was around. Mark had lost his room key, the hotel did not have a copy, and he was depressed about it. Later, I'd learn that a passenger had mistakenly taken his key to the disco and then later quietly placed it in the grass to be "found" in the middle of the night. For now, I tried and failed to cheer Mark up. My Dragoman trip ended on an anticlimactic note, with his being distracted and everyone else missing.

Chapter 18

Loop to Lalibela

This is where I am, I thought, testing out writer Karen Blixen's phrase about Africa. *This is where I ought to be.*

It didn't ring true. Ethiopia had worn me out. My travel-weary brain was barely a match for the hunger-inspired creativity of Addis Ababa's finest con artists. And while two weeks in the countryside immersed in Ethiopia's rich culture had been rewarding, as Ethiopia is one of the few African nations untouched by colonization, the downside had been exhausting. White tourists are uncommon in rural Ethiopia, and I'd been poked, touched, and yelled at on a regular basis.

"Youyouyou!" yelled the Ethiopian children every time they saw a white person. "You . . . *faranji!*"

But before leaving Ethiopia, I had decided to make one last stop at Lalibela. Lalibela, with its medieval rock-hewn stone churches, is the single don't-miss site of the African horn. I'd convinced my new friend Monica to leave the Dragoman truck and come with me on public transportation. She could wait for the rest of the group to catch up with her in Lalibela while I struck out alone toward Sudan and Egypt.

"Do you know the difference between *faranjis* and Ethiopians?" the owner of an Internet café asked, addressing Monica on our first night away from the rest of the group. We had left Axum on an early bus and arrived in the upscale Tigrean capital of Mekele after only one breakdown.

"Mmm . . . no. What?"

"When *faranjis* go out for coffee, they all pay separately."

He laughed uproariously, either at his joke or the absurdities of *faranjis*. Ethiopian custom was that the individual who did the inviting always picked up the tab.

The next morning, we were ushered through the bus-park gate before opening time. No one complained. *Faranjis* were, not unjustly, considered incapable of fending for themselves against the wild-eyed locals, who were jostling each other and pressing themselves against the gate in preparation for the mass sprint to the buses.

"Run, *faranji!* Run, run!" An old man hooted at us gleefully from his place outside the gate.

We were safely seated on the Woldia-bound bus by the time

the floodgates opened at six on the dot to let the local passengers race in. The bus seated fifty but still filled quickly, and those who arrived too late for a seat shoved their way into the aisle. Once the seats were all taken, the conductor told people to leave. Arguments ensued, as would-be passengers appeared to plead their cases to the conductor. The conductor had no doubt heard every sob story imaginable, and he motioned them all toward the door. The bus could not leave until the unhappy passengers were all convinced to vacate the premises.

Meanwhile, the usual assortment of vendors, beggars, and priests wanting alms took advantage of the delay to canvass the seated crowd. A man with no legs hopped down the aisle using his arms as crutches, pushing his way past packages and arguing people. I was surprised to see that his hands were protected with wooden blocks. I had seen legless men in Ethiopia before, but they had all worn rubber flip-flops on their hands.

Once those passengers who couldn't find seats were cleared out, we finally left the bus lot. We turned a corner to where a fence blocked us from view in the bus lot and stopped. The doors opened. A line of passengers boarded to stand in the aisle. Several of them had moments before been ejected by the conductor, who now laughed with the new arrivals and sold them tickets. The doors shut and we roared south toward Woldia. The sun came out—unrelenting as always—and the passengers around us opened their umbrellas.

"This is the first time I've seen anyone use an umbrella on a bus," observed Monica. I didn't answer. I was attempting to surreptitiously capture the Kodak moment, though I knew that the cheap point-and-shoot I'd bought in Addis Ababa would never capture the absurdity of the umbrellas-on-a-bus moment.

Our first bus breakdown occurred just before lunch. We disembarked on a dusty bumpy road to view antifreeze drenching the dirt beneath us.

Our temperamental radiator brought us to a halt several more times that afternoon, ensuring that the charm of independent travel had long worn off by the time the bus crawled into Woldia at dusk. A hotel tout named Lyuwork introduced himself to us at the bus stop.

"Do you know of anyone driving to Lalibela tomorrow?" I asked Lyuwork. If we could score a lift in a Land Cruiser, we'd get to Lalibela in four hours. The bus—if there was one—would take twice as long.

"Yes, come with me."

Lyuwork introduced us to a driver who said he had a Land Cruiser. I negotiated passage to Lalibela, and then Monica and I excused ourselves and headed to a decent hotel we'd picked out of my guidebook. We agreed to meet Lyuwork at a nearby pastry shop at eight the next morning. He was there, and so was a young church deacon who had bought the fourth seat in the Land Cruiser. But the driver was nowhere to be found.

"He will be here," said Lyuwork. "I promise."

When the driver finally showed up, he arrived in a pickup, not a Land Cruiser, to explain that our departure had been delayed.

By ten thirty, we'd given up and were trying to hitchhike out of Woldia. There had been a bus, but it had left promptly at six. My hopes of seeing the rock-hewn churches of Lalibela were evaporating quickly.

For what seemed like hours, we stood in the sun and flagged down passing vehicles. We accosted every car, truck, and donkey that stopped at the Mobil station on the edge of town. A green truck en route to Lalibela refused to stop for us because the only seats were in the back.

"It is not proper for *faranji* to sit in the back with the cargo," explained Lyuwork.

"We'll sit anywhere! We just want to go to Lalibela," I said. It seemed hopeless.

Finally, at noon, an Isuzu truck stopped at the Mobil station. The driver said the truck was going to Lalibela at 2 PM. I pleaded with him to take us along.

"If you haven't found a lift by then, I will take you."

After more futile hitching in the hot sun, we gave up. We decided to go back to the hotel for lunch and go at two in the Isuzu.

I shouldered my pack and waved down a horse-drawn carriage— the local version of a taxi. Monica and Lyuwork would wait to catch a second cart and would follow me in a minute.

I was nodding politely at the cart driver as he spoke to me in his cheerful and unintelligible Tigre or Amharic, when I saw the Isuzu truck roar by with Monica and Lyuwork in it. They honked at me and waved frantically. The Isuzu was leaving early.

"Stop!" I yelled.

The cart driver smiled happily at my excitement and continued driving the horse toward the hotel.

"No, no, *stop!*" I pretended I was leaping off the cart. Puzzled, he shook his head at me and continued.

I reached over, grabbed the reins, and tugged. The horse stopped. I leaped off with my pack, threw two birr at him, and chased after the Isuzu.

Several hands reached off the Isuzu bed to pull my pack up. I ran around to the passenger door and got in. Monica flashed me a big smile and we both laughed with excitement. We were going to Lalibela after all!

But first, we had a few stops to make.

We drove down some back streets, into the depths of Woldia. The driver parked behind another Isuzu truck. It seemed that we were going in a convoy.

Cargo was piled onto both trucks. We sat for hours as word spread through town and more and more cargo appeared. The locals stared unabashedly at us *faranji*. What were two tourists doing in the back streets of Woldia? Eating stale cookies for lunch and playing finger games with children was what, and that got boring after two hours.

Finally, in late afternoon, the loading was complete. "We are carrying one hundred tons," our driver told us. The maximum weight limit, spelled out clearly on the truck bed, was fifty.

The driver hopped in and started the engine.

"Lalibela!" I said, relieved to finally be moving.

"Lalibela!" declared the driver happily. His enthusiasm was contagious.

Ten minutes later, we were back at the Mobil station, getting gas and washing windows. After filling up, the driver moved the truck to the side of the Mobil station and disappeared into the hotel across the street. Monica and I waited impatiently until five, at which point, frantic with irritation, we decided to take action.

"I'll talk to the guy who works on the truck, and you go talk to the driver," Monica said.

I crossed the street to the hotel to find the driver. He was sitting in the backyard of the hotel, sipping tea with a friend.

"Please," I said in Amharic, pointing to the corresponding word in my phrasebook. "Lalibela." He motioned to me to sit down and made clucking noises. I refused, shaking my head. "Please," I repeated for good measure. He smiled and stared, then said "Lalibela," with a reassuring smile. He continued drinking his tea.

I went back outside, where Monica was making better progress.

The guy who worked on the truck turned out to be Mendes, the truck guard. His English was excellent, and he told Monica we were leaving at sundown. The truck was too overloaded, which meant we had to travel after dark so we wouldn't be stopped by the police.

"Overnight," said Mendes. I thought this was a reference to when we were leaving. Later, I realized he'd been referring to the duration of our journey in the slow, overloaded truck.

We waited, but our spirits fell with the sun. *Maybe we'd never leave.*

At seven, once the sun had set and the sky was dark, we finally pulled out. The driver had brought along a bag of leafy green qat, a popular chewable stimulant. At least he hadn't opened it yet. He was still "sober," I told myself as Monica and I hoisted ourselves into the cargo-heavy truck.

A new passenger had gotten up front with us too, so now we were four. The Ethiopians argued with him to get out and quit crowding the *faranji*, but he refused.

The other passengers—twenty to thirty of them—climbed onto the truck bed and perched haphazardly atop the cargo.

"Lalibela!" I declared with all the enthusiasm I could muster.

"Lalibela!" confirmed the driver.

"Name?" he asked.

"Marie," I replied.

"Monica," she said.

"Ah, Monica Lewinsky." The driver winked knowingly. This always happened when Monica introduced herself in Africa.

"City?"

"New York," I said. Monica was from Scotland.

"Ah, Osama bin Laden," said the driver. I nodded. I was used to this response by now.

We drove a few miles out of town and suddenly stopped in the darkness.

"Mendes," yelled the driver through his window. The truck guard, who was among those perched atop the cargo, slowly climbed down to appear at the driver's window.

Together, the driver and guard opened the engine compartment and took out what looked like a spark plug. They used fuel to clean it and replaced it. Beams of light cut through the darkness from the back. Every passenger save the babies seemed to be sporting a flashlight. Occasionally, one would flash past a face and we'd get a glimpse of a cheerful Ethiopian smile. Sitting on top of a sack on a clear night wasn't the worst place to be. In fact, the passengers atop the cargo seemed to be enjoying themselves.

On we went, the overloaded Isuzu struggling up Ethiopia's steep mountain roads. The headlights from the truck behind us threw our shadow—a giant truck profile dotted with heads and bodies on top of mounds of cargo—onto the cliff face.

"My Eye-suzu—fantastic," declared the driver. Monica and I politely agreed. I rolled my eyes in the darkness.

The fourth cab passenger opened the bag of qat. Monica and I watched nervously as the driver and our fellow front-seat passenger started chewing the intoxicating leaves. I tried not to think about the consequences.

"You like Kenny Rogers?" the driver asked, before inexplicably pulling out a Michael Bolton tape. I grinned, enjoying the absurdity of the moment. I was thankful the cassette deck was broken.

Hours went by as we crawled along. Monica dozed off a few times, waking whenever we drove over potholes. I stayed awake. Should our driver get drowsy, I was ready to poke him. Finally, after midnight, we turned onto a pitted dirt track.

"Lalibela Road," declared the driver.

Both he and the passenger were nuzzling closer to us in the already tight cab. I spotted Monica firmly remove the driver's hand from her knee. The other passenger leaned into me suggestively.

According to my guidebook, Ethiopian women often played hard to get even when interested in a man, so a polite "no" wouldn't necessarily do the trick. Both Monica and I were aware of this, having laughed with the Dragoman group at the section of the guidebook that explained this. We now discussed our predicament in low tones.

"How can we change this dynamic?"

"Wanna swap? That should distract them for a while."

I leaned forward and Monica scooted under me. I now sat next to the driver and Monica sat between me and the other passenger. The men only laughed and didn't hassle us again.

I tried to relax, but my left buttock was squashed against a plastic tray and a Coke bottle, and my right was squeezed up against Monica, who had been mistaken for a fluffy pillow by the other passenger.

The ride was interminable. The nighttime chill found its way in. The passenger window was permanently cracked open and rolled neither up nor down. The door and window handles were missing. We used a coat hanger to get in and out.

Finally, after more than nine hours of driving at a crawl, shimmering lights appeared in the distance.

"Lalibela Airport," declared the alert driver in his singsong voice. His words woke Monica from her fitful sleep. She sighed with relief.

Just as we contemplated the airport, and our proximity to our destination, the truck headlights cut off. All indicator lights, parking lights, and electricity shut down. We were left in total darkness. The road ahead of us disappeared.

But my luck had finally run out. The Isuzu driver panicked. He jerked the wheel to the left while hitting the brakes. The left side of his "fantastic Eye-suzu" crested over the road's slight shoulder in seeming slow motion.

On the day our Dragoman Mercedes had been bogged in the

soft gray clay underside of the Kenyan desert, Mark had mentioned the truck's "point of departure." I made a mental note to tell him that the point of departure for an overloaded Isuzu truck is about 12 degrees.

We teetered and tilted, crash-landing at a 90-degree angle, squarely on the driver's side. The driver and the other passenger were silent, stunned in the total darkness. The windshield had spidery cracks across it. A startled wailing erupted outside.

I broke the silence in the cab.

"I'm okay," I said clearly.

"I'm okay, too," responded Monica.

"Let's get our bags and get out of here. We'll walk."

"Right." Monica agreed. We'd had enough madness for one day.

The other passenger, from where he lay beside the only accessible door, made no movement.

"*Open the door,*" I ordered him with all the firmness I could muster.

"I can't," replied Monica, who assumed I'd been talking to her. The other passenger blocked her access to the feeble coat-hanger handle. For a minute, I thought we were trapped as I realized the only working door handle—on the driver's side—was now adjacent to the ground. *Would I panic? No. I was too annoyed to panic. Too sick of the whole predicament to let fear control me.*

Monica poked the passenger and motioned to him to help her. Together they lifted the door, which had become heavy in its new incarnation as a hatch.

He climbed out and turned back to help Monica climb out next. But the driver, who had been shocked into silence until now, suddenly came to panicked life. He clambered over the two of us, kicking wildly in his rush to escape. Monica and I leaned back and covered our faces, trying to avoid his erratic feet. *Let him go first. He is obviously in a rush.* He climbed over us and out, jumped off the truck, and ran away into the darkness. Perhaps he thought he had only seconds before the wailing from outside the cab turned into mob justice.

Maybe he was right. Monica and I, though blameless, needed to get away too. Emotions would be high and if scapegoats were needed, we'd be the nearest available targets.

The driver had compounded his reckless driving mistake by slamming shut the passenger door on his way out, leaving Monica and me trapped inside the dark cab once again. Monica sighed with exasperation and then tapped on the window to remind the passenger outside that we were still inside. "Remember us," she said.

He helpfully lifted the hatch and then climbed to the ground. I gave Monica a boost, and then I climbed out of the cab myself, surprised at the strength I suddenly found in my arms. Miraculously, my bike messenger bag was still intact and attached to me. My passport, money, and guidebook were inside. Monica's small knapsack was also with us, as she'd been holding it on her lap when the Isuzu had rolled.

The other passenger motioned to Monica from the ground that he would catch her, so she jumped off the truck. But he'd only half caught her, so she'd nearly sprained her ankle. I waved away his offer of assistance and climbed down carefully, finding toeholds in the side of the massive Isuzu's underside.

We walked around the truck to find a scene of chaos, lit by wavering flashlights. People and cargo were strewn everywhere, and the wailing had turned into screaming. I realized that while I was mostly annoyed by the last twenty hours, it was time to take the situation seriously. We were not only the nearest available scapegoats, we were the only ones calm enough to go for help.

No one appeared to be trapped by the cargo or the truck itself, but it was impossible to tell if anyone was actually injured, as even those who appeared unharmed were wailing incessantly. I needed to find my pack, but I worried that now was not an appropriate time to ask around about my luggage. As my eyes adjusted to the darkness, I spotted the bag. Using blades of grass, I wiped some specks of blood off the straps and shouldered the pack. I wished I had more than Dramamine and Pepto-Bismol in my first-aid kit.

"We're going for help," Monica told Mendes. He nodded. Another passenger begged us not to go; everything about this was illegal—the police couldn't get involved.

"Too bad. We're going." We strode off quickly in the darkness before anyone thought to stop us. They could have. We had only a vague idea of how to get through the black night to the distant lights.

"We'll use one flashlight at a time to save batteries," I said. We had no idea how long our batteries would last or how far away the airport actually was. Distance and the darkness itself could be deceiving.

"Right," said Monica, flipping her light off. "And drink some water. Stay calm. We must not go into shock."

We began a forced march, my eerie matter-of-fact calm slowly replaced by shakiness as it dawned on me that I'd just been in a serious accident. We both commented on mysterious pains. I felt an agonizing pain behind my left knee, a dull ache in my left ribs, and a stiffness spreading along my calf and thigh. Monica's pain was in her shoulder and neck region. But we didn't want to stop to examine our injuries. It didn't matter if they were serious; we still had to get to the airport. Whatever damage had been done to us could wait. We needed to get help while putting distance between us and the emotionally charged crash scene.

Just before we stumbled over an unexpected bridge, a small old man draped in a blanket materialized out of the dark and into our circle of light. He may have heard the crash, or the wailing, or he may just have seen a flashlight and two *faranji* coming down a dark road at nearly five in the morning.

I opened my Ethiopian phrasebook to the "Emergency" section in the back.

"There's been an accident," I pointed out. "Danger. Emergency."

"Eye-suzu," added Monica, while I pivoted my arm 90 degrees down from the elbow.

The man nodded his comprehension and strode off in the direction of the truck accident.

As he went, he emitted several shrill yelps. A minute later, similar yelps echoed back and forth across the fields. People sleeping in their darkness-hidden huts woke up and started the march over to the crash site. The man was raising the alarm. It reminded me of the "Twilight Barking" in *101 Dalmatians*. I was impressed at the time, although Mark would later point out, "Now there would just be more people standing around staring."

Monica and I stumbled across the bridge and came to a crossroads. A sign—in English for tourists—indicated that the airport was to the left, but Lalibela itself was to the right. We looked both ways and hesitated. "Perhaps we should go to Lalibela," I suggested.

"But there will be someone at the airport, and they will have a radio," said Monica. "And we can actually see it from here." I agreed and we headed left. We were lucky we chose the airport. Later we discovered we would have had to walk many miles into the mountains to get to Lalibela.

Adrenaline was pushing us on, giving me the ability to ignore the pain in my ribs and leg. I didn't even feel the weight of my forty-pound pack, which seemed to float along with me as if filled with helium.

But as pain made it increasingly difficult to ignore my injuries, it occurred to me that it would do me no good to bleed to death. I paused and pointed my flashlight at my wounds. The back of my knee featured a deep puncture wound, and a massive dark purple bruise spread along the outside of my calf and thigh. I had a sharp chest pain that I chose to ignore as a less immediate problem. Monica's neck was sore, but she was still moving. She'd fallen only against me, but I'd fallen against the gearshift, the plastic tray, a Coke bottle, and the driver.

We walked our forced march through the blackness for an hour, passing Ethiopians en route to the crash scene. They did not seem surprised to see us. There were no phones out there, but word seemed to have traveled quickly by yelp-telegraph.

At last we reached the airport gate. A uniformed guard came out to greet us. I showed him my phrasebook lines and said, "Eye-suzu." He motioned us on down the driveway toward the airport itself.

"Hey," he yelled after us. We paused. Perhaps he needed more information.

"Cigarette?"

"No," said Monica, who had a pack of cigarettes in her pocket. *What the hell was the matter with that guy, slowing us down when people's lives were at stake?*

A lazy-eyed soldier wearing an AK-47 and a blanket approached us outside the terminal. We explained about the crash, again supplementing our limited language with my phrasebook. He woke the other soldiers, who were asleep on cots in the guardhouse. They dutifully paid attention while he explained the situation.

"Call ambulance," I suggested, pointing at the words and wondering if perhaps they couldn't read. I mimed talking into a phone.

They didn't move.

"Many people dead?" asked one tentatively.

"I don't know," I shrugged. *Why weren't they springing into action?*

One of them went somewhere, possibly to radio in the emergency. Or maybe he just went to pee.

"Two hours," said a soldier. *Two hours what? Until the ambulance got there? Until the airport opened? Until the local Red Cross arrived?*

Then we realized why the soldiers weren't reacting. They had no vehicle, and I assumed there was no ambulance in Lalibela. There was no one to call.

The soldiers escorted us into the closed airport and stood outside the ladies' room while we were allowed a moment inside.

Both Monica and I inexplicably had a brief moment of hysterical giggling over a stray turd that floated listlessly inside a toilet bowl. For a minute, I thought I was going to throw up. Then I recovered my composure. *I'd made it this far on eerie calm and exasperation. There was no point in losing it now.*

We were escorted back to the guardhouse, where the guards just stared and didn't seem to know what to do with us. Monica and I sat down on a concrete barrier and turned our backs to them. I could feel my temperament cooling, my panic of a minute ago seeping out to be replaced by relief. My left leg ached and stiffened as the bruise spread its way up my thigh and blackened. I continued to ignore the pain in my chest. Maybe it would go away. The puncture wound behind my knee now made its presence known by stinging and demanding my attention. I wiped it with a Wet One.

"Monica," I said. "What is the point of travel insurance?"

She laughed, a little louder than she usually laughed. Like me, she had comprehensive travel insurance with medical evacuation coverage. But we now knew that all the coverage in the world wouldn't do us a bit of good once we were beyond the reach of cell phones and emergency services. If either of us had been seriously injured in the Isuzu accident, we would be dead regardless of our health coverage.

Our good luck now apparent, we settled in to wait for the airport employee bus that was due at eight. The bus would take us to town, to view our grail, the rock temples of Lalibela. We shared a granola bar I'd found in my pack and quietly contemplated the Ethiopian sunrise.

Chapter 19

Suddenly Sudan

"Are you going to Sudan from Shihedi?" asked the bus conductor. "Follow me. A white man has just come to Gonder from the border yesterday. He is here to catch a bus this morning."

Shihedi was forty kilometers east of the Ethiopian border town of Metema. Rumor had it that there was a decent hotel in Shihedi, but that "nothing" was in Metema.

The "white man" turned out to be a Japanese backpacker.

"There are, um, *simple* hotels in Metema," said the backpacker ominously. "But you *must* go there to catch a lift north to Gedaref. It could take you several days as few trucks go through to Sudan."

Gedaref was the first major town in Sudan, and one I was legally required to visit to apply for Sudanese travel permits. I didn't have "several days," as I needed to be on a Europe-bound ship out of Israel on November 23—just more than a week away. I hoped the backpacker was exaggerating, or that he was simply unlucky. But I had to consider what he said. No published guidebook even mentioned this route, and the only information available was from other travelers, both live and on the Internet.

Worried, I returned to my bus to find it was full. I squeezed around the other two in my seat—three to a seat was common in much of Africa. Our bus roared out of the fenced-in bus lot, leaving the paved roads of Gonder behind and plowing down a dirt track westward toward the border. Ethiopian reggae played on the driver's cassette deck, and as usual, we stopped frequently in small towns that were little more than collections of stick huts. Everyone stared at me, smiling curiously, and I retreated into my own mental space.

The twenty-year-old man sitting next to me—quiet at first— bought some *kolo* from a young female vendor who boarded the bus at one of our short stops. He offered me some. It looked brown, hard, and seedlike, and it tasted like burned popcorn.

He turned out to speak fluent English, having learned it from a missionary in Sudan when he'd been a refugee there. During the Ethiopian civil war and war with Eritrea, many refugees had been sent to Sudan, including my mother's former foster daughter. Sophie had found her way to the States (after a run-in with the law in Sudan for having worn shorts). She had remained in America after aging out of the foster-care system but some Ethiopians had returned to Ethiopia once it was at peace.

"Stay in Shihedi," recommended the young man, who made frequent trips to Shihedi to show videos for a small admission fee. "The hotels in Metema are not suitable for you. At eleven tomorrow morning, catch the Isuzu to Metema. It is only one and a half hours. At Metema, catch a lorry to Gedaref, where there is a paved road and a fast, new bus. You could be in Khartoum tomorrow night."

I knew that eleven Ethiopian time was 5 AM by my standards. Ethiopians measure the day from daybreak, so their "one" is our 7 AM. And I knew that a lorry was British English for a truck, and I also knew that it was quite improbable that I would be in Khartoum that easily and quickly. Nothing in Africa went as smoothly as the man described.

The bus trip to Shihedi was over a bad but not intolerable road, and the journey was only six hours long. I laughed at how my standards had changed. Six hours in a packed bus was comfortable compared to a lot of trips I had taken this year.

A Metema-bound bus was waiting at Shihedi, but I went with local advice and checked into the blue and pink hotel behind the bus lot.

"It is the best hotel in town," said my self-appointed guide. "It has a good shower." He left me in a small concrete cell with a single open window. There was no blanket, but I was still carrying my sleeping bag. I showered under the famed shared spout, ordered an Ambo, Ethiopia's superb brand of seltzer, and settled into the hotel's front room to listen to the sounds of Shihedi.

The click of a pool queue on billiard balls came from next door.

The *Xena: Warrior Princess* war cry came from outside, indicating a sporting event was on, or that the girl's choir was practicing. Traditional Ethiopian music sounds a lot like Xena going into battle.

Ethiopia had been all right in the end. It had as rich a culture as anywhere I'd ever been, and the touts were less aggressive and more pleasant than in many regions. In spite of my near-death overturned-truck experience of thirty-four hours earlier, I was happy to be there. The shocking purple-black bruises on my left knee and thigh reminded me of a certain gearshift as well as of my fantastic luck to date.

Still, it was time to move on. Ramadan started in two days, and I needed to get to Khartoum before the Muslim world took a holiday.

Everyone I asked in Shihedi had a different opinion about how to get to Metema—there were trucks, I could hitch, there might be buses— but in the end a scheduled morning bus carried me to the border.

"Good morning, Mare-ee," declared the bus driver. He'd stayed in the same hotel that I'd been in and we'd met over dinner. "We're late." He laughed and started the bus.

As usual, I was assaulted by kindness as the bus motored onward. Little girls outside mud huts hooted and waved, men in remote villages hopped on at stops to try out their English and my Amharic, and everyone stared gleefully at the blond tourist in their midst. No one yelled "youyouyou" at me here. I was so far off the beaten path that I was a complete novelty.

At Metema, the bus staff gently steered me to Immigration. After brief Ethiopian border formalities (conducted in a hut), I shouldered my pack and began the hot ten-minute walk across no-man's land into

Sudan. Ethiopians traveling the same route hired carts with donkeys to carry their luggage.

"*Salaam aleykum,*" I addressed the assembled Sudanese officials at the border. To my relief, my visa was in order and the Sudanese let me in. I was trading the creative, overwhelming chaos of Ethiopia for the rule-based structure of northern Sudan. The south was the war front in a decades-old devastating civil war that would end in January 2005 (only to have a conflict then crop up in the west), but the northern half of Africa's biggest country operated by a stringent set of Muslim laws. As long as I didn't break any, or get involved in any political discussions, I should cruise through quickly to Egypt.

Dozens of people had warned me not to go into post-September 11 Sudan. "It's full of terrorists," wrote MariesWorldTour.com readers. "You'll be kidnapped! You'll be killed!" It was the first and only time I flagrantly ignored the will of the readers. They'd overwhelmingly voted for me to fly to Egypt or to sail around Sudan. But as an American abroad on September 11, I felt a responsibility to culturally interact with people in Muslim nations and to demonstrate a lack of terror. My contribution to world peace was microscopic, but I could offer a smile and a few pleasantries in place of paranoia. It wasn't much, but I told myself that if more of us were out in the world interacting, it would go a long way toward showing that Americans were willing to engage the world on a local level.

If there were one single lesson that I had taken from my yearlong ground-level journey around the world, it was that the vast majority of people are friendly. Governments may fight, but individuals are overwhelmingly willing to deal with each other on a personal level.

Religious, cultural, and governmental differences tended to vanish as soon as people spoke to each other one on one.

On my website, I had preached a lot about engaging the world, and now was the time to "put up or shut up." Global engagement and cultural understanding—not isolation—had been a part of my mantra long before I'd left my job and traveled the world. I put on long sleeves, covered my head with an Ethiopian scarf, and climbed into the back of a tattered Bedford cargo truck bound for the deeply rutted dirt track to Gedaref. Trucks left frequently. The Japanese backpacker had been wrong.

A young Ethiopian woman and a grandmother bought the two places in the front cab seat in the truck, leaving one Ethiopian man and forty other Africans of various nationalities to climb into the back with me. Fifty hours after surviving an overturned cargo truck, I was back in the same risky circumstance, with no alternative. And this time I wasn't even riding in the cab but in the hot "seat," crunched between sacks of grain, charcoal, garlic, and a mother with a dehydrated, listless baby.

Every time we hit a pothole or bump, I (along with everyone else) became airborne. Upon landing, my bruised ribs ached sharply. A Muslim man dressed in a long white cotton robe and trendy sneakers grabbed my arms and hauled me back into the truck every time I seemed to be about to fly away. A knee was in my back, a crotch by my ear, and I was putting my hands in inappropriate spots on other people. My butt was wedged between two sacks and my underwear hung out for all to see. *So much for Muslim modesty,* I thought. Another passenger relinquished his more stable seat on a sack, motioning me into it after I fell over and nearly crushed an infant.

The point of departure of a semioverloaded Bedford truck, I noticed, was much higher than the point of departure of a severely overloaded Isuzu. We didn't crash, despite tilting precariously in all directions.

One passenger stared aghast, his mouth open in disappointment, when his plastic bag of garlic burst open. Garlic bulbs spread everywhere, so I supplied him a green plastic garbage bag I'd carried from Kenya. I was carrying a few in anticipation of a dusty train ride through northern Sudan. It came with its own pull-tie. The man thanked me and then scrambled to collect his garlic while the group murmured its admiration of the bag.

They call this a road? I thought, wincing from the sharp pain in my ribs as I landed on my pack again. Everyone grabbed for available handholds. The mother with the listless baby tried to give the child water and winded up dousing the infant.

We banged and clattered along our filthy, dusty way for ninety kilometers. It took five hours. We were lucky. In the rainy season, the same trip had taken Australian writer Peter Moore three days.

Darkness fell after we passed the outpost-like town of Dokka. From my perch on my backpack, with a Sudanese woman's arms on my thighs and an Ethiopian man using my wristwatch as his own, I stared at the stars. My friends the Sudanese didn't care that I was American, or that the United States had just renewed sanctions against their country. We were all in this filthy, bumpy, hellish stew together.

At nine, someone poked me and uttered "Gedaref." Ahead were

the lights of a small city. The young Ethiopian woman from the truck's front seat ushered me into Gedaref's Ethiopian Compound—a fenced-in area with a concrete building in the middle, several beds in the yard, and two pit toilets in the corner—for the night. I slept inside on a rickety, metal bed. The two Ethiopian women shared a single bed, sleeping head-to-toe. The men slept outside, under their own sheets, their beds covered in mosquito nets.

I'd been hoping for a hotel room and a long shower. Instead, "Mother," the older Ethiopian woman from the Bedford (all Ethiopians seem to call older women "mother"), poured a pitcher of water over my head while I scrubbed. We couldn't communicate at all—she spoke Tigre and my limited Amharic was useless. She'd talk to me in sign language—she showed me when she liked something by patting her chest, told me to put on sleeves by motioning to my wrists, and let me know when I could take off my head scarf by tugging at it.

We were served *fuul*—a Sudanese meal of beans and cheese scooped up with bread—and sugary tea. I supplied wet wipes to my new friends. They accepted them gratefully, but the younger woman put hers aside for later. She was disappointed then to find that it had dried out.

I spent half the next day filling out forms and haunting officials while encouraging them to issue my travel permits. It was four by the time a taxi driver deposited me on a large, new, purple luxury bus bound along paved roads to Khartoum.

The air-conditioning kicked in along with a recording of the Koran.

Staring out the window as the parched desert landscape whizzed by, I watched donkeys pulling carts to the rivers, where women filled barrels with water. Rural residents were decked out in *Titanic* T-shirts—someone Stateside must've given a massive inventory to charity. Mud huts dotted the desert. But, surprisingly, so did telephone poles and electrical wires.

At six, bus attendants handed out dinner trays. I stared at mine, mocking me beneath its plastic wrap. I hadn't eaten a proper meal in days. I'd had some Ethiopian chickpea mush back in Shihedi, a peanut butter sandwich yesterday morning, and a little *fuul* in Gedaref. But it was Ramadan and the sun was still up. I'd have to wait. *For God's sake,* I thought, and then laughed at my choice of words.

Finally, just before six thirty, there was movement. Grinning at my attempted holiness, the Sudanese man next to me nodded permission. I could eat now.

And I did, tearing into my bread and chicken with gusto. My standards had changed during the past eleven months, and bus food now seemed quite appealing.

Just before seven, we pulled into a disorganized huddle of shacks and small buildings. This was the edge of Khartoum, itself merely a larger collection of huts, shacks, and concrete blocks, albeit mixed with a few embassies and luxury hotels.

"Danah Hotel," I told a taxi driver. The Danah had been listed in a copy of *Africa on a Shoestring* I had borrowed from a Bosnian tourist back on the TAZARA train from Zambia to Tanzania.

"Five thousand dinar," said the driver after delivering me as promised. I looked at him in horror. He pried five hundred dinar from my hands and waved goodbye.

The Danah was friendly enough. The clerk was versed in passable tourist languages, including English. The rooms had telephones and CNN. The showers, while not hot, were not freezing. I happily stood in one, letting the cold water rinse away the filth of Ethiopia and the Sudanese desert.

My plan for my Sunday in Khartoum was to visit the spot where the Blue and White Niles converged, to see the Antiquities Museum, and to travel a few hours north to the town of Meroe to visit its ancient pyramids. On Monday, I'd catch the rickety old train for the dusty fifty-hour ride to Wadi Halfa, where I'd catch the weekly ferry to Egypt.

Instead, after a lazy day enjoying expensive juices and a Western lunch in the nearby Hilton lobby, I spent two days vomiting in the shabby Danah hotel room in Khartoum. Later, I'd discover that the Ethiopian truck accident had left me with more than bruises. I had at least one cracked rib, which led to walking pneumonia. At the time, all I knew was that I seemed to be catching every respiratory and flulike illness in Sudan.

At the end of my second day of feverish delirium, a BBC producer tracked me down through my website. *Everywoman* was doing a special on "women on the road."

"What were some of the highlights of your trip?" asked the interviewer.

All I could think of was my flu, the Isuzu accident, and starving during Ramadan in Khartoum. I thought of the confusing Sudanese tendency to quote prices in thousands when they meant hundreds. I thought of anonymous dead men lying by the road in Ethiopia, and of children demanding pens in Tanzania. I forgot about canoeing past hippos in Zimbabwe, barreling down sand dunes in Namibia, and watching the stars amid Filipino seamen on the *DAL Kalahari*. Gone were the pre-Africa highlights: the race for the bug-eating gold in China, performance art in Berlin, and pony-riding across the Mongolian Steppe. I blathered something inadequate about Ethiopian Orthodox culture and hung up to mull over my poor articulation abilities in private.

The ferry to Egypt left once a week—on Wednesdays. My *Grimaldi* freighter to Italy left Israel in four days, on November 23, and the QE2 liner was picking me up in England on December 10. I'd used my travel days being sick in Khartoum, missing the once-weekly train as well as any buses. I now had no choice but to fly to the ferry.

At what point does a trip around the world without *airplanes become a trip* with *airplanes?* I asked myself. I was flying for the second time in a week, the first flight having been from Lalibela to Gonder, a town with modern medicine and licensed doctors, the same day the Isuzu truck I'd been riding in flipped over. Of course, bruises and broken ribs hadn't stopped me from having a quick look at Lalibela's rock-hewn churches. I'd gone to enough effort to get there and didn't want to miss the sights.

I'll just have to redefine the trip, I thought ruefully as I got out of bed on Wednesday morning. I had failed in my mission, but I had a hard time considering my trip a failure. Writer Bill Bryson, I reasoned, had not succeeded in hiking the Appalachian Trail but still made a successful story out of it with his book *A Walk in the Woods.*

The bruises on my left side were dramatic but fading. My fever had subsided, and my tummy roar turned into just a slight ache. My left rib cage still hurt, but with time (and the aid of an Italian physician), that would lessen.

The small, Russian-built Sudanese Airways plane left me at the parched, sandy town of Wadi Halfa. I got to the port, acquired a ticket (and the necessary exit permits), avoided a mandatory yellow-fever shot by brandishing my medical certificate, and boarded a small, rickety ferry for the voyage to Aswan.

It is only a twenty-hour overnight trip, I thought. I was so close to Europe now. I could take whatever Sudan could dish out.

A thin Egyptian official with a lazy eye ushered me aboard and left me sitting alone on a bench in Second Class. First Class had been sold out, but Second Class didn't look so bad. It was a series of large rooms filled with wooden benches. I spread out my stuff.

But then more and more passengers boarded, and a tolerable trip turned into a potentially hellish ride.

This won't do at all, I thought, as the fourth passenger sat down to share my bench. Would all four of us sleep sitting up on the slatted benches?

The nearby toilets were making their presence known, emitting a powerful odor of urine. I'd taken my head scarf off and it now covered my nose.

It's squalid hell, I thought grimly as I reviewed escape routes. I had none. No trains, buses, or planes were scheduled to leave Wadi Halfa for seven days. The foul ferry was my only way out.

How ironic, I thought. That same afternoon, the BBC had

been singing my praises about what a tough worldly traveler I was. Meanwhile, I sat in squalid hell, dizzy from urine fumes and likely to cry from discomfort.

Then the Marlboro Man walked in. His horse, a Yamaha motorbike with Sudanese license plates, sat in the hallway. He was ten days younger than me, was the only other non-African on board, and was riding his bike from Sudan to Munich after spending two years teaching auto mechanics in western Sudan for the German Development Service. Later, he'd tell me that the Sudanese had pointed me out to him and said he should "go to his sister."

"Hello," said the sandy-blond–haired, rugged Marlboro Man. "I'll talk to you later." He walked off, leaving me surprised and speechless. *Was that attractive man in his sister's brown leather biker pants a mirage?*

He wasn't. He caught up with me shortly after the ferry pushed off, when I bolted for the deck and the outside air.

"I'm going to take my sleeping bag out on deck later," he explained in his Bavarian-Sudanese-English accent. "If I'm quiet, maybe they won't mind."

I decided then and there that I was joining him whether he liked it or not. Squalid hell would have to make do without me.

We scouted out the deck and found two crates to perch on.

"See that?" I pointed to the roof of the bridge. "It's Monkey Island. We'll sneak up there after dark."

He agreed to give it a try. On most ships, Monkey Island—or the flying bridge—is accessible only by a ladder and is always windy. Since we were the only two people on board with sleeping bags, we'd have no competition for Monkey Island.

A young Egyptian man I'd met in Khartoum dropped by to relay the horrors of the northward train journey I'd missed while sick, and to practice English. He was polite enough to ask our names (something I'd quit doing months ago), and that is how I learned that Herr Marlboro's name was Werner.

Werner spoke passable Arabic and every Sudanese man on board seemed eager to test it. He was immensely popular with his light hair, motorcycle, and Arabic. Relieved to be in the audience for a change, I sat and watched the banks of man-made Lake Nassar, created in 1968 by damming the Nile at Aswan.

The call to prayer sounded after six, and the faithful gathered in a row to kneel toward Mecca. Because of physical space constraints, this meant we had a row of men chanting "Allah Akbar" at our feet. We kept quiet and tried not to giggle disrespectfully.

The Sudanese started turning in early. Piles of men in white cotton robes and hats littered the deck, curled up together like cats, presumably for warmth. One such pile of men lay at the bottom of the ladder to Monkey Island.

"New plan," I said. "We're going to have to scale the wall." It wouldn't be difficult. The wooden crates put us halfway there. We'd camp out under the stars, curling up together like the Sudanese men.

I was as dazzled as the Sudanese and Egyptians by this tanned man speaking crazy English and worse Arabic. We talked for hours under the stars. I neglected to mention the Australian waiting thousands of miles away for me. Werner neglected to mention the nurse he thought was waiting for him in Germany. Neither would matter to us in a few years, or a few weeks in his case. I would snuggle up against him that night, and he'd curl a leg over mine. I wouldn't care that I was bruised and sick, or that I had no chance of riding off into the sunset on the back of this Bavarian man's motorcycle. All I knew was that while no kiss was given or offered, and while no plans were made to meet again, sleeping next to this stranger under the stars on the Nile was the single most romantic night I'd ever experienced.

Werner and I stayed up late, until we passed Abu Simbel, with its magnificent tombs that had been saved by UNESCO. Piece by piece, they'd been dismantled and reassembled on higher ground. The statues were lit at night, something I'd missed when I'd visited them on a day trip from Aswan two years earlier. The sight of them filled me with relief. We were in Egypt, land of the pharaohs, the tourist, baksheesh, the leg-groper, and the Big Mac. After four months in Africa and seven months in Asia, Australia, and Europe, I was practically home.

Acknowledgments

Thanks to friends and family who helped me get off the ground and running. My mother, Steve Buccellato, Marie Alice Arnold, Jonathan Babcock, Richard Starkings, and John "JG" Roshell made my round-the-world trip possible. Warren Ellis occasionally sends readers my way. Yancey Labat, Don Hudson, and Kevin Kobasic contributed art to my site.

Thanks to the following businesses for their support: Comicraft/ Active Images, Comiculture, Adventure Center, Internaves, Nomad Adventure Tours, Crazy Kudu, Thebe River Safaris, Shearwater, Zambezi Safari and Travel Co., Audi Camp, Guerba, Dragoman Overland, Grimaldi Lines, Cunard.

Thanks to these people for helping me out in Africa: Shawn Marshall, Paul Franklin, Marky, Sammy, Monica Hoey, my fellow Dragoman passengers, Celsius, Peter Moore for Sudan visa advice.

Special mention must be made of Herr Marlboro, who was deeply involved in the early stages of this book. The hippo is not the only wild animal in Africa that I needed to escape. Thanks to my family, Nikki Hall, Edward Readicker-Henderson, Sean Henry, Shannon Wheeler, Ed Ward, Rachel Chiu, Michael Kraiger, Polly and Al, Roberta Melzl, Helen Whitehead, Sue Crespi, and Jessica Wolk-Stanley for support when I needed it most in Namibia in 2005.

Thank you to Brooke Warner at Seal Press for her leap of faith, and my eternal gratitude goes to Karen Bleske for her tireless, sensitive editing. Thanks to Turbo for unceasing support—until it ceased—but the kudos go to Niclas Holm in Sweden. Though we'd never met, he read each chapter as I wrote it in Kuwait and offered boundless encouragement by SMS and email.

Thanks also to everyone mentioned in this book, my pals in Kuwait, the friends I met along the way, everyone on my mailing list, and especially those who wrote back.

About the
Author

Marie Javins is a writer and editor who left a fun-filled job at
Marvel Comics to go around the world by local transport in 2001,
blogging all the way on MariesWorldTour.com. She is the author of
The Best in Tent Camping: New Jersey (Menasha Ridge Press, 2005)
and a full-time freelancer who colors and edits for Marvel Comics,
Gemstone Comics, and Kuwait's Teshkeel Media Group. Originally
from Northern Virginia, Javins considers herself a New Yorker but
has lived in Australia, Barcelona, Uganda, Namibia, New Jersey, and
Kuwait over the last five years. She can say "hello," "thank you," and
"how much" in seven languages.

Selected Titles from Seal Press

For more than thirty years, Seal Press has published groundbreaking books. By women. For women. Visit our website at www.sealpress.com.

Es Cuba: Life and Love on an Illegal Island by Lea Aschkenas. $15.95, 1-58005-179-0. This triumphant love story captures a beautiful and intangible sense of sadness and admiration for the country of Cuba and for its people.

Mexico, A Love Story: Women Write about the Mexican Experience edited by Camille Cusumano. $15.95, 1-58005-156-1. In this thrilling and layered collection, two-dozen women describe the country they love and why they have fallen under its spell. Also available, *Italy, A Love Story: Women Write about the Italian Experience*. $15.95, 1-58005-143-X and *France, A Love Story: Women Write about the French Experience*. $15.95, 1-58005-115-4.

No Touch Monkey! And Other Travel Lessons Learned Too Late by Ayun Halliday. $14.95, 1-58005-097-2. A self-admittedly bumbling vacationer, Halliday shares-with razor-sharp wit and to hilarious effect-the travel stories most are too self-conscious to tell.

Pirate Queen: In Search of Grace O'Malley and Other Legendary Women of the Sea by Barbara Sjoholm. $15.95, 1-58005-109-X. A fascinating account of one of history's most intriguing women, along with tales of cross dressing sailors, medieval explorers, storm witches and sea goddesses.

The Risks of Sunbathing Topless: And Other Funny Stories from the Road edited by Kate Chynoweth. $15.95, 1-58005-141-3. From Kandahar to Baja to Moscow, these wry, amusing essays capture the comic essence of bad travel, and the female experience on the road.

The Unsavvy Traveler: Women's Comic Tales of Catastrophe edited by Rosemary Caperton, Anne Mathews, and Lucie Ocenas. $15.95, 1-58005-142-1. Thirty bitingly funny essays respond to the question: "What happens when trips go wrong?"